SECURITY RISK: PREVENTING CLIENT VIOLENCE AGAINST SOCIAL WORKERS

■ ■ ■

Susan Weinger, PhD

NASW PRESS

National Association of Social Workers
Washington, DC

Ruth W. Mayden, MSS, LSW, *President*
Toby Weismiller, ACSW, *Interim Executive Director*

Cheryl Y. Bradley, Director, Member Services and Publications
Paula L. Delo, Executive Editor
January Layman-Wood, Acquisitions Editor
Robin Bourjaily, Copy Editor
Deborah E. Patton, Indexer
Mia Reese-Smith, Editorial Secretary

Library of Congress Cataloging-in-Publication Data

Weinger, Susan.
Security risk : preventing client violence against social workers / Susan Weinger.
    p. cm.
Includes bibliographical references and index.
ISBN 0-87101-321-5 (alk. paper)
    1. Social workers—Crimes against—Prevention 2. Violence in the workplace—Prevention. 3. Social servics—safety measures. I. Title.

HV40.35 .W45 2001
361.3′2′0684—dc21   00-053318

■ ■ ■
CONTENTS

··· ABOUT THE AUTHOR

Susan Weinger, PhD, is associate professor of social work at Western Michigan University. In addition to working on safety issues, Dr. Weinger conducts research focusing on marginalized populations and global social work issues. Her background includes over fifteen years of clinical social work practice in mental health facilities and public school settings.

■ ■ ■

INTRODUCTION

Social service agencies and individual social workers often take measures to increase employee and personal safety only after there is a violent incident that causes serious injury. Social workers work with clients in close relationships in which they try to understand how clients feel about their experiences. Because of our feelings for clients, it is difficult to consider that one of them might hurt us. Perhaps it is not surprising that as a profession we have been reluctant to address and implement safety procedures.

This manual is written to enable social workers to consider safety before a calamity occurs. The best way to manage violent behavior is to prevent it. To do so, we must be mindful of the possibility and warning signs of violence, and we must prepare ourselves to think clearly in these emergency situations. Then we will be able to use the sensitive communication skills developed in our profession to more likely avoid and de-escalate potentially violent situations. Although we work to serve others, we cannot do that well when our own safety is being violated. Therefore, we need to formulate policies and structures that reduce our risk.

Safety cannot be guaranteed through any training manual, agency, or supervisor, or even through competent social work skills and conscientiousness. Even though we cannot ensure 100 percent safety, we can certainly do our utmost to reduce the risk of violence. Because this has not been a focus of our profession before now, today we have an urgent need to make safety issues a priority. When there are incidents of violence, we must learn from these situations, support our distressed colleagues, and further develop our responses and interventions to protect each other, our clients, and ourselves. This manual was written to advance us toward achieving these goals.

The manual has many uses—as a guide for social workers in the field, as a resource for agencies or organizations, or as a framework for courses and continuing education workshops. It is also designed to serve the needs of social work students as part of a formal orientation to fieldwork. Requiring specific participation in a safety training session apart from the regular curriculum may ensure that every student receives similar coverage of this material. However, it is also possible to build safety training into field seminars and practice classes.

This book is, for the most part, geared to the individual student or practitioner rather than to an instructor or workshop class. Readers will notice that role-plays and group discussions are suggested in several sections of the book. If co-workers or fellow students are available, conducting such activities may be extremely valuable, but these are not crucial to understanding the material or learning from it.

This manual also provides an overview of safety issues. In addition, each practitioner or student needs training and information specific to her or his particular agency or practice site.

I want to thank Drs. Linda Reeser, Kenneth Reid, and Philip Popple and members of the former Safety Committee at Western Michigan University for their support and input during the initial phase of this project.

Susan Weinger, PhD

■ ■ ■

ORGANIZATION AND OBJECTIVES OF THIS MANUAL

This book comprises five chapters. Each chapter is divided into sections that begin with **Section Goals**, which identify what teaching points the section's material hopes to convey, and **Getting Ready**, which proposes preparation or enrichment activities that may aid in the understanding of the topics that follow. Each section concludes with **Points to Remember**, which encapsulate the main ideas of the material just read. Additional materials mentioned in the sections are located at the end of each chapter.

The objectives of this manual are:

- To encourage students and social workers to be more alert to and mindful of safety issues.
- To provide information about how to detect the potential for physical violence.
- To allow students and social workers to consider alternative responses in potentially dangerous situations.
- To help students and social workers understand the application of communication skills in some situations of potential danger.
- To introduce safety awareness in the physical, organizational, and policy structure of social service agencies.
- To introduce discussion of issues in the aftermath of violence.

1

■ ■ ■

INCIDENCE AND UNDERSTANDING OF THE VIOLENCE DIRECTED TOWARD SOCIAL WORKERS

Section 1: Dilemma, Incidence, and Reasons for Increasing Violence toward Social Workers

Section Goals:

- To help students and social workers realize that being alert to safety should not distance them from clients.
- To help students and social workers understand that safety is an important issue for practitioners today.
- To consider the reasons social workers are sometimes at risk.

Getting Ready:

- Complete the **Introductory Questionnaire** at the end of the chapter.
- Take a moment and reflect upon your response to:

Question #1: What do you hope to learn about safety issues for social workers?

Which of the objectives on page ix most closely parallels yours?

DILEMMA

Question #2: How do you think our efforts to use safety measures in our work might affect the way we think about clients?

Safety training presents a dilemma for social workers. On one hand, social workers need to learn about safety issues, because the frequency of assaults on social workers is rising. We cannot serve as sacrificial lambs; we have a right to safe work environments and need such surroundings so that we can be effective in our work. Yet safety training may affect our orientation and attitude toward the clients we serve. If we must mentally respond to safety-related questions before we have contact with clients and use various technological gadgets to protect ourselves, might these measures create distance and polarization between us and our clients? Ironically, if safety training contributes to a reduced understanding between worker and client, then perhaps the worker may be more likely to become the victim of violence by being less attuned and empathic to the client. Such a dilemma does not preclude safety training. It suggests that while we strongly impress on ourselves, our colleagues, and students the need for safety considerations in the face of rising assaults on social workers, we also need to undergird our training with an understanding of the wider issues and causes of violence.

INCIDENCE

Question #3: How important an issue do you think safety is for social workers?

There is limited social work research measuring the extent of violence perpetrated against social workers. Case examples and some empirical data suggest that the incidence of client violence toward social workers is increasing (Newhill, 1995).

Physical violence by clients against workers is more likely to occur in certain settings, such as in agencies dealing in health, mental health, and services for people with disabilities. Verbal threats from clients are especially common in correctional facilities (Schultz, 1989). Patients who are likely to be out of control during stays in inpatient settings make the number of assaults on clinicians more likely (Guy & Brady, 1998). But as managed care necessitates less frequent and shorter inpatient stays, incidents of violence in outpatient and private practice settings appear to be increasing dramatically (Guy & Brady, 1998). Although some studies report violence occurring more often in particular practice areas, it appears that the frequency of violence is mounting in all social work settings (Newhill, 1995). This is so even as under-reporting is suspected, due to lack of institutional reporting policies and social workers' fears that their victimization will reflect badly on their professionalism (Occupational Safety & Health Administration [OSHA], 1996).

OSHA announced in 1996 that "more assaults occur in the health care and social services industries than in any other" (OSHA, 1996, p. 2). Another source specifies that half of human service workers will experience client violence at some point in their careers (Blumenreich & Lewis, 1993). Though these statistics are not broken down between medical personnel and social workers, or between degreed social workers and persons employed in social services positions, it is a justifiable conclusion that graduating social work students today will be more likely to face violent confrontations than their counterparts 25 years ago. Indeed, new research appears to indicate that at least a quarter of social workers will confront a violent situation at some time on the job. A 1996 study that surveyed social workers found that 23 percent had personally sustained a physical assault by a client at some point in their career, while 63 percent indicated that a co-worker had been physically victimized (Rey, 1996). Two earlier studies found respectively that two-thirds of a random sample of social workers in West Virginia had been physically assaulted by a client (Schultz, 1987), and 24 percent of field instructors at the University of Georgia experienced physical violence at least once in their career (Tully, Kropf, & Price, 1993).

Often attacks do not result in physical injury or involve a weapon. Guy, Brown, and Poelstra (1990) reported that only 30 percent of clinicians attacked sustained any physical injury and only 10 percent described their injury as more than moderate. Furthermore, it appears that most attacks consist of hitting, biting, kicking, scratching, or choking the clinician and do not involve a weapon. Usually the violence is not premeditated; if a weapon is used, it frequently is an object available in the immediate surroundings, such as a book, phone, or ashtray (Guy & Brady, 1998).

Students and new social workers may be more vulnerable than experienced practitioners (Guy & Brady, 1998). Some studies indicate that less experienced practitioners are more often targets of clients' violence (Carmel

& Hunter, 1991; Guy & Brady, 1998; Star, 1984). However, two studies found them less likely to be targets or found no correlation between experience and victimization (Farber, 1983; Tully, Kropf, & Price, 1993). If students and less experienced clinicians are more vulnerable to assault, this may be because they set fewer limits, allowing more acting-out behaviors to escalate into aggression. Or they may not be as adept at anticipating patient behavior and responding to it as effectively (Guy & Brady, 1998). Whether or not they are more vulnerable, social work students are exposed to potential violence in their field placements. A study pertaining to violence in field placements found that both BSW and MSW students reported experiencing verbal abuse (Tully, Kropf, & Price, 1993). Surveyed MSW students reported client violence as one of their top three practice concerns in their field placements (Newhill, 1995).

The reports of growing violence toward social workers and the indication that social work students in their field practice are not exempt from danger motivated the development of this safety manual for both students and experienced practitioners. Regardless of work setting, client population, and worker experience, any practitioner can be a target of client violence. Because many incidents of client violence tend to be random and impulsive, they are not predictable. Thus, the potential of client violence is real for all clinicians (Guy & Brady, 1998).

REASONS FOR INCREASING VIOLENCE TOWARD SOCIAL WORKERS

Question #4: Why do you think that social workers might be victims of client-perpetrated violence?

1. *Inadequate Mental Health Services for the Potentially Violent*
   The deinstitutionalization movement has left many persons with mental illness at risk by disbanding services in state hospitals without providing compensatory community mental health services. Furthermore, with managed care there is pressure for infrequent and briefer periods of hospitalization. Many patients are released without appropriate follow-up care. Legal issues surrounding hospitalization, discharge, and administration of medication also contribute to the development of incendiary situations. Protection of client rights has enabled patients to refuse treatment and also to refuse psychotropic medications. While

persons with mental illness are generally no more likely to be violent than the rest of the population, mental illness is a complicating factor when combined with other risk factors (Brown, Bute, & Ford, 1986; Newhill, 1992, 1995).

2. *Social Control Roles for Social Workers and the Negative Image of Social Workers*

It can be argued that in all fields of social work practice social workers have long employed social control strategies. Even in private practice, clinicians necessarily set limits and use gate-keeping measures. Such potentially therapeutic as well as social controlling maneuvers as these can provoke anger in nearly all contexts in which social workers serve. However, social workers are now carrying out even more obvious social-control activities as the result of relatively recent legislation and court orders (Griffin, 1995; Newhill, 1995). With the passage of child-abuse acts and elder-protective laws, social workers have become mandated reporters, active investigators, and even vigorous pursuers of sexual abuse perpetrators. These more authority-based functions expand into custody and divorce settlements, domestic violence situations, involuntary hospitalization, and suicide prevention (Rey, 1996). Social workers carry out court orders in relationship to treatment for driving under the influence (DUI), welfare fraud investigations, the *Tarasoff* decision, and abortion clinic operations.

By intervening in situations that are very volatile and concern highly personal and emotionally wrenching matters, social workers may become the focus of clients' anger and resentment. The community's image of social workers has moved from helpers toward representatives of unwanted authority (Griffin, 1995; Schultz, 1989). Furthermore, the public has increasingly reported incidents of child abuse and domestic violence, only to be discouraged that social workers do not immediately solve complex relational problems (Griffin, 1995).

3. *Cuts in Services and Provisions*

Social workers are often on the front lines during this conservative period of cutbacks in social services and provisions. Programs for poor people, community resources, and outreach have been steadily reduced. Many individuals and families live below the government's poverty line and experience little hope for the future. Working within a shriveling system, social workers can be easily blamed for the longer wait to receive help and for denials of needed services (Griffin, 1995; Schultz, 1989).

4. *Increasing Violence in Society*

The greater violence prevalent in society makes social work practice more dangerous. More clients have histories of violent behavior; there is increasing violence by female clients and the elderly. Greater substance abuse and the prevalence of handguns are associated with the frequency and severity of assaults (OSHA, 1996). The growing criminal justice system cannot keep pace with the rising criminal population. Correctional facilities on the average have been unable to rehabilitate or confine the criminally violent or to curb recidivism (Bouza, 1993).

Reasons cited for America's "culture of violence" include racism, prejudice, sexism, political and economic policies that trap people in poverty, weakened values and lack of cohesion in the community fabric, socialization of men to be aggressive, glorification of violence in popular culture, and easy access to guns (Kemper, 1993). The chief of the Washington, DC, police force, a veteran of 28 years of service, declares, "The time has come for politicians and society alike to bite the bullet, to trade easy responses for real solutions, to get angry enough and compassionate enough and smart enough to address the cause of violent crime: poverty, guns, drugs, and a value system that is totally out of kilter" (Kemper, 1993, p. 70).

Points to Remember:

- We need to make safety concerns a priority in our professional lives, being careful not to impair the empathic nature of our relationship with clients.
- The incidence of violence toward social workers is increasing in all settings.
  - Particular settings may have higher rates of violence, but violence is not restricted to particular settings or client groups.
  - Violence is rising even while underreporting is suspected.
  - OSHA reports injuries from assault highest in health care and social services.
- Students may be more vulnerable to assault than experienced workers, but any clinician can be a victim of violence.
- Reasons for increasing violence toward social workers include:
  1. Mental health services for the potentially violent are inadequate
     - Deinstitutionalization without compensatory community mental health services

- Medication refusal by discharged patients
- Treatment refusal

2. Social control roles
   - Expansion of social control roles for social workers places them in the middle of potentially explosive circumstances.
   - Social workers (seen as purveyors of authority rather than as helpers) have a tarnished image.

3. Cuts in services: Governmental cuts in services and provisions increase client frustration with social workers.

4. Growing societal violence is evidenced and promoted by
   - Increase of violent acts by women and elderly people
   - Substance abuse
   - Prevalence of handguns
   - Conditions that breed hopelessness and desperation, for example, racism, sexism, economic oppression, and a breakdown in shared values and interconnection
   - Socialization of men to be aggressive
   - Societal reinforcement and glorification of violence.

Section 2: Understanding Violence

Section Goals:

- To present different ideas about the causes of violence, noting the need for various types of responses
- To emphasize that one cause may be disequilibrium in power
- To conceptualize the occurrence of violence in a person-in-environment framework

Getting Ready:

Think about these questions, "Is violence inevitable to human beings? Is it a part of human nature? Is it learned? Is it an outcome of life's frustrations? Is it driven by society?"

UNDERSTANDING VIOLENCE

Question: **Is violence inevitable to human beings? Is it a part of human nature? Is it learned? Is it an outcome of life's frustrations? Is it driven by society?**

Causation Hypotheses

One major hypothesis of violent behavior contends that it involves intrapersonal events, while others attribute its development to interpersonal and external influences.

1. *Innate Aggression*

   Psychoanalytic theory considered aggression an inherent part of human nature. Freud conceptualized that impulses toward aggression are innate and build up if they are not permitted some direct or circuitous means of discharge. This destructive drive may express itself through violent behavior if it is not sublimated or otherwise transformed (Wistedt & Freeman, 1994). Lorenz also viewed aggression in humans and in other animals as an instinct rather than as a response to any environmental stimuli (Brown, Bute, & Ford, 1986). This instinctual aggression grows until it is released by aggression–releasing stimuli (Wistedt & Freeman, 1994). The body has an arousal system of biological reactions associated with violent actions, including a triggering of hormones and a rush of chemicals producing a "natural high."

   Implications of instinct theories are that "persons need to let off steam," perhaps by throwing darts, punching a boxing ball, or watching violence in the media (Brown, Bute, & Ford, 1986). While some social scientists maintain that this idea is true, others contend that it has not been supported. A contrary view is that watching aggressive sports and media violence may desensitize us and increase the likelihood of assaults (Brown, Bute, & Ford, 1986). Nevertheless, these theories direct social workers to channel inevitable client aggression into less damaging actions.

2. *Social Learning Theory*

   Albert Bandura, a leading figure in the development of social learning theory, conjectured that an individual cannot display aggressive behavior unless she or he learned it by direct experience, usually through watching others (Norris, 1990; Wistedt & Freeman, 1994). This theory proposes that it is not biological imperatives but social learning that determines how people will act on their feelings. People learn to channel their emotions into attacking outbursts by witnessing this behavior in others and also from observing and experiencing that aggressive behavior gets rewarded. Teachers, parents, subcultures, and the wider society model and promote aggressive behavior through the use and sanction of corporal punishment of children in some of our schools and through child abuse and spousal abuse in many of our families. One of the most consistent findings in psychological research is that children who are disciplined by physical punishment are more likely to become aggressive adults. Television, cartoons, comics, and films reinforce the teaching that violence is a common, admirable, and efficient means through which to get power, control, and attention (Brown, Bute, & Ford, 1986).

Social learning theory implies that what can be learned can be unlearned through new learning. If the environment provides consequences or sanctions for violence that are not desirable, the person can unlearn acting violently. Furthermore, the person may learn alternative actions for expressing anger.

3. *Frustration Leads to Aggression*

Persons experience frustration when they perceive obstacles blocking their progress toward their desired goals. Anger is a normal response to frustration. When continually blocked from achieving an expected goal or reward, an individual may get enraged and express this anger violently in an attempt to remove the obstacle (Hart, Broad, & Timborn, 1984). Frustration cannot explain all violence, however, because some perpetrators do not experience frustration before their aggression. Furthermore, obstacles and hassles are a part of life, and many persons cope with their frustrations without resorting to violence. Other negative reactions to frustration besides violence include "restlessness, tension, destructiveness, apathy, fantasy, regression, and the adoption of repetitive, fixated behavior" (Brown, Bute, & Ford, 1986, p. 36). Many people dealing with expected frustrations of life are able to control their angry feelings. The violence-prone individual, however, may be overwhelmed by frustration and unable to tolerate the lack of need-gratification (Hart, Broad, & Timborn, 1984). Thus, while frustrating circumstances may provide an impetus for clients to react with rage, frustration is not the sole explanatory cause of violence.

4. *Violent Societal Structure Creates Violent Expression*

Gil (1996) asserts that human nature is both violent and nonviolent; which behavior is expressed depends on the social structure in which human nature develops. Humans are nonviolent when their intrinsic human needs are fulfilled so that they can develop in healthy ways and actualize themselves. Conversely, Gil states that people behave violently when their inherent human need to develop their potential is obstructed by the social conditions in which they live. When institutional systems deprive people of their inherent needs—such as material necessities, social relationships, a sense of belonging, respected and productive work, and so on—then people's natural energies to develop constructively and fulfill their potential are blocked. Consequently, this developmental energy is channeled into destructive, violent expressions. Rather than seeing acts of violence as reflective of individual or group deficiencies and as separate, disconnected events, this viewpoint regards such violent reactions as inevitable responses to historically entrenched exploitative social conditions.

All four theories have heuristic value. A person who becomes aggressive may have weak inhibitions (innate aggression), have used violence "successfully" in the past (social learning theory), and have confronted an excessively frustrating environment (frustration leads to aggression), perhaps because of subjugation and domination by more powerful people or groups in the social hierarchy (violent societal structure).

Violence Occurs in Context

The social work perspective of person-in-environment helps us consider the occurrence of violence through a broad lens that leads to practice implications. Rather than viewing certain persons as inherently violent, we can understand most violent behavior as an interaction between the person's internal dynamics, the interpersonal situation, and the environmental system. Although anyone can become violent or aggressive, persons differ in their speed and tendency to convert aroused emotions into behavior. Some persons have a shorter fuse and less internal capacity to modulate feelings, self-sooth, and express emotions verbally. Violent behavior erupts from the interactive combination of these internal features, along with situational and interpersonal factors (Sheridan, Henrion, Robinson, & Baxter, 1990). Even though a person may have a shorter fuse or be more prone to violence, the immediate context influences whether that fuse gets further ignited or quelled. This gives social workers the ability to use knowledge and skills to defuse potentially violent situations.

Disequilibrium in Power Triggers Violence

Violent behavior can be regarded as a defensive reaction to a perceived threat or expectancy of harm. Fear initiates anxiety, which may be converted into anger. If anger is not dealt with in other ways, it can ignite into aggressive behavior. By becoming violent, an individual can get temporary relief from extreme feelings of anxiousness and helplessness. Anger may be a more comfortable feeling than torturing anxiety; aggressive behavior provides a brief sense of power (Hart, Broad, & Timborn, 1984).

Accordingly, an angry, aggressive attack by a client toward a social worker may be triggered by a disempowering encounter. Violence may stem from a "disequilibrium of power" and serve as "a final way of restoring balance" (Kaplan & Wheeler, 1983). In one study psychiatrists reflected on incidents of patient violence toward them, and over half revealed that a power struggle preceded the assault (Madden, Lion & Penna, 1976). For example, they had turned down a patient's request, were too intrusive in their interpretations, or had set limits inappropriately. Persons who have not had power over their lives may be very wounded by perceived slights to their self-esteem, status, and reputation. Enraged reactions may be in retaliation for such insults, pain, and humiliation, and an attempt to capture some of the power and control denied (Star, 1984).

No Proscriptive Response

Understanding the human needs underlying violent expression gives social workers direction as to how to intervene (Boettcher, 1983; Brown, Bute, & Ford, 1986). Though this manual will focus primarily on violent communications stemming from angry aggression, social workers need to be aware that there are other types of aggression. Sources of aggression include biological and physiological bases. Organic brain disease can be a cause of violent behavior. Following a head injury, resulting confusion and irritability can cause a person to be more prone to violence. Organic brain disorders such as delirium and dementia make violent behavior more likely (McNiel, 1998). A person with antisocial personality disorder may use aggression as a calculated means to achieve her or his satisfaction, with limited compassion toward others or little sense of social responsibility. Also, a person may present potential danger by acting on a paranoid delusion.

Depending on the underlying causes or motives for the aggressive communications, we may need to intervene in ways to equalize power and help someone talk out feelings, to set very firm convincing limits, or to reassure the client and help her or him receive emergency medical care. There is no formulaic response for handling all possible volatile situations. The complexity of each individual situation must be taken into account to create

11

appropriate, specific responses. Indeed, more research is needed to recommend and justify certain responses to specified types and causes of aggressive behavior. In the meantime, it may help clinicians in thinking through their responses during a potentially violent incident to have considered possible ways to become aware of dangerous situations and to explore a variety of alternative responses in advance.

Points to Remember:

- Four major notions of how persons become aggressive-prone individuals are:
  1. Aggressive impulses are innate and build up if blocked.
     - Physiological changes occur during violent episodes.
     - Nondestructive activities are needed as an outlet for this inherent aggression.
  2. Aggressiveness is socially learned through observations and rewards.
     - A great deal of societal modeling and rewards for violence occur.
     - Corporal punishment of children is linked to aggression in adulthood.
     - Violent media teach that violence is status enhancing.
  3. Frustration leads to aggression.
     - Persons get frustrated when blocked in reaching their goals.
     - Aggression is not the only reaction to frustration, so it is not an all-encompassing explanation for aggressive behavior.
  4. Social conditions that create powerlessness breed violence.
     - When persons are powerfully blocked from meeting their survival and human needs, their energies are channeled into destructive, violent expressions.
- Social work perspective views violence as erupting in context rather than being stored within the "violent individual."
  - Immediate context influences whether the client's fuse gets ignited.
  - Since the immediate context is important, social workers may be able to use their skills to have some influence on deterring violence.
- Disempowering encounters may trigger violence.
- Aggression can stem from different human needs.
- One way of interviewing does not fit all needs.
- This training is not all encompassing; it is a beginning.
- Social workers need to flexibly consider various ways of responding.
- Learning about safety needs to be ongoing.

INTRODUCTORY QUESTIONNAIRE:
INCIDENCE AND UNDERSTANDING OF VIOLENCE

1. What do you hope to learn about safety issues for social workers?

2. How do you think our efforts to use safety measures in our work might affect the way we think about clients?

3. How important an issue do you think safety is for social workers?

4. Why do you think that social workers might be victims of client-perpetrated violence?

2

. . .

RECOGNIZING
POTENTIAL VIOLENCE

Section 1: Recognizing Dangerous Situations

Section Goals:

- To identify signals for assessing a potentially dangerous situation.
- To reinforce the need to be conscious of and heed gut-level feelings that warn of impending danger.

Getting Ready:

Think of a client signal, an environmental signal, and an internal signal that might point to a dangerous situation.

RECOGNIZING DANGEROUS SITUATIONS

When social workers have heightened awareness of the potential for violence, there is an opportunity to rapidly assess the likeliness of its occurrence and intervene early. It is important to stay alert to possible signs of danger, taking in signals from the client, from the environment, and from within ourselves.

CLIENT SIGNALS

Social workers should be alert for any of the following signals listed in Table 2.1 from their clients:

TABLE 2.1. Client Signals to Consider when Assessing Risk

SIGNAL TYPE	EXAMPLES	SOURCES
Body movements	A great deal of activity, exaggerated movements, pacing, tense muscles in hands and limbs, shifting positions, rocking, flailing arms, jerky nonfluid movements, threatening gestures, clenched fists, wringing hands, pounding of fists on a table	Flannery & Penk, 1996; McNiel, 1998
Speech	Loud, sharp, pressured speech	Flannery & Penk, 1996; McNiel, 1998
Facial cues	Muscle tension in the face, gritting teeth, dilated pupils, scowling, staring, glaring, flushed, inappropriate affect, pale	Hart, Broad, & Timborn, 1984
Bodily changes	Sweating, shakes, tremors, trembling, heavy breathing	Flannery & Penk, 1996; McNiel, 1998
Agitation	Easily excited, quick responses to stimuli, hyperactive, appears tense or ill at ease, overly anxious, easily upset when things go wrong, hypervigilant, sweating	Flannery & Penk, 1996; McNiel, 1998
Angry verbalizations	Sarcastic, complaining, challenging, insults, swearing, impulsive, or threatening statements	Flannery & Penk, 1996; Hart, Broad, & Timborn, 1984
Emotional distress	Unhappy, distressed, irritable, emotionally labile, negative, lying, suspicious, uncooperative, hostile	Flannery & Penk, 1996
Thinking difficulties	Disorganized, confused, disoriented, persecutory ideas, hallucinations	Flannery & Penk, 1996; McNiel, 1998
Signs of intoxication	Lack of coordination, slurred speech, unsteady gait, fluctuating levels of consciousness, dilated pupils, flushed face, tremors	McNiel, 1998

ENVIRONMENTAL SIGNALS

The following clues in the environment may tip off the social worker to a potentially violent situation:

- Are there clients and others who could get hurt in the vicinity?
- Are there persons who would serve as an inciting audience?
- Are colleagues present who could be available for assistance?
- Are there any obvious weapons or objects that could be used as weapons?

INTERNAL SIGNALS

While working with clients, social workers should remain aware of their own internal responses:

- What are your own inner reactions?
- Do they give you any indication of potential danger?

The social worker's own feelings often provide crucial warnings. Tune into such feelings and give them credence. Clinicians who know themselves well will be better able to stay in touch with their own feelings and thoughts and can utilize these internal reactions to assess possible danger (Guy & Brady, 1998). Many times after a violent incident, workers admit that they had dismissed feelings of being threatened (Hart, Broad, & Timborn, 1984; Whitman, Armao, & Dent, 1976). De Becker (1997) also reports that even though intuition powerfully and swiftly discriminates myriad nuances, giving humans a sense of fear that is accurately predictive, victims of violence often ignore their intuitive fear. Perhaps behind this is the worry that acknowledging the risk will make it happen, while denying danger will magically cause it to vanish. Sometimes it may be tempting to disregard intuition if the reason for fearful feelings cannot be explained logically (De Becker, 1997). However, it is important to break through denial and *pay attention to gut-level feelings.*

Although denial can impede taking action based on intuitive warnings, constant hypervigilance may interfere with the recognition of real danger signals. If social workers are always afraid and perpetually alert "it becomes impossible to separate the survival signal from the sound bite" (De Becker, 1997, p. 296). It is more effective to give credence and attention to intuitive warnings of the presence of danger than to be on permanent guard.

As social workers, then, we must tune in to our own feelings not only to warn us of potential danger but also to help avoid unintentionally communicating something that would increase the likelihood of violence (Guy & Brady, 1998). If we are aware of our own feelings, we can thoughtfully choose to communicate them or another message that may be more appropriate for the client or the situation. A client's perception of a worker who inadvertently communicates hostility, anger, or tension may trigger an attack (Blumenreich & Lewis, 1993).

Although heeding intuition has been stressed as critical, it comes with a caution. The validity of intuition can be marred if it is heaped with cultural biases or misinformation. Body language, facial gestures, and verbal expressions may communicate different meanings across cultures. Not taking these cultural differences into account may result in disregarding serious danger signals or erroneously intuiting them to be present.

Additionally, it is important to know our own professional competencies and limitations so that we can seek support and help before a situation develops into a violent crisis. By assuming responsibility for keeping safety concerns in the foreground, practitioners can stay alert to circumstances and reactions that might escalate over time.

Points to Remember:

- Assess danger signals coming from
  - the client
  - the environment
  - within yourself.
- Gut level feelings may provide crucial warnings; stay in touch with them.

Section 2: Predictive Individual Factors

Section Goals:

- To familiarize students or social workers with the correlates of violence in a way that lessens preconceived prejudices.
- To highlight that the best predictor of violent outbursts is a history of violent acts.

Getting Ready:

Consider the following question, "What client characteristics would you look for in the record that might indicate the potential for violence?"

PREDICTIVE INDIVIDUAL FACTORS

Prediction is not an exact science; each practitioner must assume responsibility for remaining aware. Detecting potential violence is not an exact science; even experienced practitioners cannot accurately predict the occurrence of violence (McNiel, Sandberg, & Binder, 1998; Newhill, 1992). Human behavior is often unpredictable, and a violent incident can flare up without warning or provocation. However, it is possible to assess risk to some extent by knowing those factors associated with the increased likelihood of violent behavior.

Client Characteristics

Question: **What client characteristics would you look for in the record that might indicate the potential for violence?**

1. *History of Violence*
   The most powerful predictor of violent outbursts is a history of violent expressions (Edelman, 1978). One study indicates that recidivists are responsible for half of the assaults on mental health workers (Blumenreich & Lewis, 1993). Persons with a criminal record or a history of violent reactions have a greater chance of being violent again. Absence of a history of violence, however, does not rule out the potential for violence.

   It is important to know the circumstances surrounding and precipitating the client's past violent actions and the similarities to the current situation. It is crucial to read client records *prior* to meeting with a client. If there is an account of repeated violent outbursts, practitioners need to know this. Records, however, are neither totally objective nor offer a complete picture. They may reflect the perspectives of the writer and agency as well as the client. The records need to be read with professional discrimination for obtaining valuable information and for generating pertinent questions.

2. *Mental Illness*

The relationship between mental illness and the tendency toward violence is a controversial topic (McNiel, 1998). On the one hand there is evidence that persons with mental illness are generally no more likely to be violent than the overall general population (Newhill, 1992). On the other hand, studies have shown that some patients or clients are more at risk of behaving violently compared to others (Guy & Brady, 1998; McNiel, 1998; Tardiff, 1997). Diagnoses of schizophrenia, antisocial personality disorder, and borderline personality disorder have been linked to violence-proneness. Persons with schizophrenia experiencing paranoid delusional thinking and hallucinations may behave violently in response to beliefs that someone is trying to hurt or persecute them (Tardiff, 1997). Persons with antisocial personality disorder characteristically show no remorse or guilt because they have not internalized moral prohibitions against violence (Tardiff, 1997). Persons with borderline personality disorder may act violently in an impulsive manner after perceiving rejection (Tardiff, 1997). Other disturbances and syndromes have been coupled with violence, such as organic brain disease/structural brain damage, mood disorders, mania, panic disorders, head trauma, and substance abuse (McNiel & Binder, 1995; Norris, 1990; Tardiff, 1997).

Though findings that connect diagnoses with violence have been mixed, there is much evidence associating acute symptoms with heightened short-term risk of violence (Link, Andrews, & Cullen, 1992; McNiel, 1998). Individuals showing high levels of hostility, suspicion, agitation, and thought disturbance are more likely to be violent no matter what their diagnosis (McNiel, 1998).

Clients with a wide variety of diagnoses, not just those mentioned, may behave violently. Keeping up to date on research findings may help social workers be aware of and yet at the same time not exaggerate any association between diagnostic categories and symptomology with violent behavior. This willl help prevent any tendency toward personal prejudices against individuals with mental illness or particular psychopathologies.

In any case, mental illness in and of itself is not a good predictor of violence (Blumenreich & Lewis, 1993). Violence is usually caused by multiple factors. If a particular illness or symptomology predisposes the individual to aggression, such predisposition must usually be combined with other facilitating components such as substance abuse, a frustrating environment, and the like to precipitate a violent outburst (Blumenreich & Lewis, 1993).

3. *Substance Abuse*

Substance-related disorders strongly increase the probability of violent behavior (Blumenreich & Lewis, 1993). Alcohol intoxication facilitates violent occurrences in two ways: It lowers inhibitions of those with a proclivity toward violence, and it interferes with their judgment (Edelman, 1978). However, alcohol withdrawal also is problematic because the disorganization and delirium that accompany withdrawal can precipitate violence (McNiel, 1998). The grandiosity, agitation, suspicion, and delusional beliefs brought on by drugs such as cocaine, PCP, and amphetamines increase the violence risk (McNiel, 1998). The euphoria associated with cocaine intoxication, especially when taken as crack or intravenous cocaine, can rapidly change into irritability, agitation, suspicion, and violence (Tardiff, 1997).

4. *History of Child Abuse*

An individual who has been a victim of child abuse or witnessed abuse at home when growing up is more likely to manifest violent behavior later in life (McNiel, 1998).

5. *Demographics*

Certain client characteristics are associated with a greater likelihood of future violence. These are: age (between 15 and 40 years) and gender (male), weapons possession, previous criminal record, and military combat experience (Hatti, Dubin, & Weiss, 1982; Newhill, 1992, 1995; Star, 1984).

Although males are more likely to attack clinicians than females, a few recent studies show that females are more likely to be physically assaultive than previously thought. One study, for example, showed that female psychiatric inpatients perpetrated more physical attacks, but male patients engaged in more fear-evoking behavior such as threats and property damage (Binder & McNiel, 1990). Another study found that female former patients of an emergency psychiatric service engaged in violent behavior with the same frequency but less severity than did the males (Newhill, Mulvey, & Lidz, 1995).

Social support can either increase or decrease the probability of being violent depending on the nature of the social network. Estroff, Zimmer, Lachicotte, and Benoit (1994) found that patients who were married or who had a mental health professional in their social network were less likely to perpetrate violence. However, some social support can actually increase the likelihood of violence, such as a family with habitual patterns of violence, or a gang encouraging a client to act violently (McNiel, 1998).

There are three caveats to note when considering characteristics associated with violence. First, although knowing the predictive factors may increase awareness, there are many false positives. Persons who do not resort to violence may also have these risk factors (Star, 1984). Second, in fueling the flames of racism we have often linked violence and crime to race. Although research has demonstrated that when different groups live in the same social, economic, and political environment their rate of violence is comparable, we have not always absorbed these findings into our mind-sets. Because of these distortions, for example, a social worker may too readily suspect an African American client and may overlook the warning signs exhibited in contact with a White client. Indeed, some studies have found that when treating patients with acute mental illness, clinicians tended to underestimate the risk of violence in female patients and overestimate it in patients of color (Lidz, Mulvey, & Gardner, 1993; McNeil & Binder, 1995). It is important for us to be aware of our own prejudices so that we do not distort our perceptions of the signals of danger.

Finally, there is a potential to use predictors of violence in a way that will create more risk to the clinician. If clinicians forsake their level of alertness because a client doesn't meet the criteria for potential risk factors, they may overlook important signals. It is important to realize that a client who presents or does not present risk factors can exhibit assaultive behaviors.

VICTIM'S CHARACTERISTICS

Few correlations appear in the literature between clinician characteristics and the likelihood of being a target of violence, and even these are tentative. This is a further indication that a violent attack can happen to any clinician; all must be alert to personal safety issues.

A few studies have shown that clinicians with an internal locus of control, who tend to be self-blaming and look to themselves when things go wrong, are less often victims of violence than those who believe that their environment controls what happens to them (Chaimowitz & Moscovitch, 1991; Ray & Subich, 1998). Holding themselves responsible, they may convey nonblaming attitudes toward the client and be less likely to experience assaults. By holding such a perspective these clinicians may also assume more responsibility for their own safety and take preventative measures.

The majority of research studies suggest that clinicians who approach clients in an authoritarian manner have a greater probability of experiencing violent episodes with clients. Authoritarian postures and attitudes and attempts to overcontrol may exacerbate clients' feelings of powerlessness, anxiety, fear, and low-self esteem, precipitating violent reactions (Kronberg, 1983; Ray & Subich, 1998).

The gender of the clinician does not appear to be associated with risk. Several studies found no difference in the degree or frequency of client assaults directed at male and female clinicians (Guy & Brady, 1998; Guy, Brown, & Poelestra, 1990; Tyron, 1986).

Points to Remember:

- The best predictor of violent outbursts is a history of violent acts.
- Other correlates are:
  - mental illness (controversial)
  - substance abuse
  - a history of child abuse
  - youth, male, weapons possession.
- Predictors include false positives.
- Our racial prejudices may misinform us about actual predictors.
- Inappropriately relying on predictors can impede safety.
- There are few correlations to victims' characteristics.
- An internal locus of control and nonauthoritarian manner may lessen the risk of being a target.

Section 3: Risk Factors Exercise and Degree of Dangerousness

Section Goals:

- To explore risks present in realistic case situations.
- To help students and social workers consider various precautionary measures.

- To promote flexible thinking and consideration of alternative actions by noting that there is usually not just one way to approach potentially dangerous situations.

Getting Ready:

Read the five case scenarios at the end of the chapter. If co-workers or fellow students are available, prepare to discuss the scenarios with them.

RISK FACTORS EXERCISE

Whether alone or in a group, determine the risk factors for each of the five scenarios at the end of the chapter and consider what precautions might have been taken. Risk factors can include such things as being isolated in a wing of the agency, client history of violence, presence of many potential weapons, an unknown client, and so on. As much as we would like to have a simple formula to ensure safety, case situations have many nuances and variables and defy simplistic prescriptions.

Points to Remember:

- We need to consider potential risk factors as we do our jobs.
- No one can ensure our safety; we have to take a responsible, active role on behalf of our own safety. This includes having the flexibility to choose an alternative behavior appropriate for the specific situation.

Section 4: Assessment Interview

Section Goals:

- To familiarize students and social workers with focus issues for assessing risk factors.
- To assist students and social workers in turning these guidelines into actual questions and observations during a simulated interview.

Getting Ready:

A helpful activity for assessing risk factors is to conduct a role-play in which a fellow student or co-worker takes on the role of a potentially violent client while others do a group interview to assess the potential for violence. Following the role-play, those present should discuss the degree of risk uncovered through the interview process, referring to the 13 suggested areas for exploration listed in Table 2.2.

ASSESSMENT INTERVIEW

In assessing a client for potential violence or interviewing a client who is known to present problems of violence, a number of areas may provide useful information for judging risk. Although there are several risk-assessment instruments, none have shown substantial predictive accuracy. Thus, we need to rely largely on our clinical assessment skills during the interviewing process. All social workers should develop their own interview questions to assess the potential for violence in accord with their own interviewing style and work circumstances (Eddy, 1998). The clinician must use clinical judgment to determine when and how to utilize such questioning and to what extent. Newhill (1992) recommended that her guidelines be used when a client has a history of violence or is in an agitated or threatening state.

The following are suggested areas for exploration taken from several sources but primarily incorporating the interview formats of Newhill (1992) and Eddy (1998).

Newhill (1992) recommends that questions be interrupted by sincere supportive statements from the worker. Reactions of the client should be carefully watched so that the worker can quickly provide calm support at the first indication that the client is getting provoked. Of course, it would not be wise to continue the interview if danger is sensed.

Points to Remember:

■ Assess the potential for violence by exploring the issues suggested.
■ Notice the client's reactions to the interview process and intervene accordingly.
■ Role-playing the interview process aids in learning to formulate questions and exploring the pertinent issues.

TABLE 2.2. Issues to Explore when Judging Risk

ISSUE	CONSIDERATIONS/APPROACHES	SOURCE
Client appearance	Tense, irritable, limited attention span, verbally aggressive, facial expression, eyes, speech patterns, tone of voice, loudness, gang signs, or scars from fighting	Blumenreich & Lewis, 1993; Eddy, 1998; Newhill, 1992
Your own feelings	Are you apprehensive, nervous or fearful with this client?	Eddy, 1998; Newhill, 1992
Potential for involvement in violent behavior	Question the client directly and nonjudgmentally, similar to the manner that you would use to question her or him about substance abuse. Has the client ever hurt herself or himself or others, made suicide attempts, used threats, or been arrested? What is the degree of past injuries to self and others? Who was involved? What happened? What were the contextual circumstances? Has the client been involved in violent behavior recently (last 6 months)? Engaged in any destruction of property, criminal offenses, reckless driving, impulsive and unprotected sexual acting out, and other impulsive behaviors?	Eddy, 1998; Newhill, 1992; Tardiff, 1997
Violent thoughts and plans	Does the client have violent thoughts or impulses? Does the client think about harming others and seeking revenge? Does the client hold grudges? If the client makes any threats, explore how planned and realistic these are. Note toward whom they are directed. Is there availability of weapons or means to inflict injury? Access to firearms? Has the client been trained in the use of firearms? Been in the military?	Eddy, 1998; Newhill, 1992

History of family violence	How were children disciplined in the family of origin? Was the client or siblings abused? Did parent(s) or other adults ever assault each other? Were the children combative toward each other? Were any members arrested?	Eddy, 1998
Childhood violence	Did the client engage in fighting behaviors as a child? To what extent? Did the client as a child exhibit cruelty toward pets?	Eddy, 1998; Newhill, 1992
Social support	What kind of social support does the client have? Who is available to the client? Are persons in the social network supportive or hostile? Does the client have a stable living situation? Does the client have a stable job situation that is reinforcing of self-worth? Does the client have a dependable job history or one that is marred by disciplinary measures and suspensions?	Eddy, 1998; Newhill, 1992
Situational and environmental stressors	Is the client going through any recent losses and stresses such as job loss, financial difficulties, or loss of significant others? What coping and problem-solving skills is the client utilizing to cope with these stressors? Are recent stressors present in combination with poor coping and problem-solving skills that could trigger an assault?	Blumenreich & Lewis, 1993; Eddy, 1998
Substance abuse	What is the client's drug of choice? How often does the subject use? How much? Additional substances? What role did substance use play in the client's violent behaviors?	Eddy, 1998; Newhill, 1992; Tardiff, 1997

(Table continues)

TABLE 2.2 (continued)

Issue	Considerations/Approaches	Source
Disordered thoughts	Note any delusions or hallucinations that convey that the client feels threatened or under the control of another. Does the client perceive that thoughts are inserted into her or his head? That others are trying to hurt the client? Does the client think that her or his mind is being dominated by forces outside of her or his own control? What would the client do if she or he came in contact with the person(s) suspected of doing this to her or him? Does the client think the clinician can hear the client's thoughts or put thoughts into the client's mind? Such thoughts can create insecurities and misunderstandings in the interview and precipitate violence.	Eichelman, 1996; McNiel, 1998
Responses to treatment	Has the client received treatment in the past voluntarily or involuntarily? What were the degree of compliance with and results of such treatment? Present compliance or noncompliance?	Eddy, 1998; Tardiff, 1997
Self-control	Explore the client's perception of her or his own capacity to control her or his own behavior.	Newhill, 1992
Mental disorders and medical problems	Are any mental disorders present, such as mania, paranoid schizophrenia, antisocial personality disorder, etc? If the client has been violent or appears potentially violent, ask questions about the presence of any medical conditions that make people prone to violence. Has the client been medically evaluated? If not, a physical exam is necessary to rule out a medical etiology.	Eddy, 1998; Eichelman, 1996; Newhill, 1992; Tardiff, 1997

PREDICTIVE FACTORS

- History of Violence

- Mental Illness

- Substance Abuse

- History of Child Abuse

- Demographics

CASE SCENARIOS: RISKS AND PRECAUTIONS

Read each of these case scenarios, one at a time. Then discuss or consider:

- What risk factors are present?
- What precautionary measures would you take?

1. You are making a home visit to a parent of a child who is in foster care to obtain permission for some procedures.

   The parent's apartment is upstairs over a storefront, reached by a long flight of narrow stairs. At the top is a short, dimly lit hall with two doors. You knock on the door. A middle-aged man opens the door. He is wearing work pants and a sleeveless T-shirt. He is unshaven and smells of alcohol. You tell him who you are and why you are there. He sways on his feet and seems confused. His speech is slurred.

2. You come out of a downtown building where you have just made a field visit. It is raining, so you pause in the doorway to pull up the hood of your coat. A young woman waiting by the door says that her ride is late and asks you to take her home. It is cold and raining. You agree to give her a ride and she follows you to your car. She indicates that she lives in an adult foster home four or five blocks away. She begins asking personal questions: Where do you work? Do you come here often? Where do you live?

3. You are a protective service worker who last night investigated a report of child abuse and neglect. You found a nine-month-old baby alone in the house and removed the infant.

   Today, the mother comes to your office, and she is very angry and upset. Her voice gets louder and louder so that people in adjoining offices can hear. The mother tells you that you had no right to remove the child; that it wasn't the agency's business; that she wasn't gone very long. Then she declares that the child is an incarnation of Jesus. She speaks in this vein for several minutes. You realize that you are sitting behind a desk with the mother between you and the door.

Several of these vignettes were contributed by or adapted from suggestions from Lethonee Jones, professor emeritus, School of Social Work, Western Michigan University.

4. At the start of the session with a new client, she informs you that she carries a gun in her purse because she feels unprotected. You ask the client if she thinks it is necessary to bring the gun into the counseling session. She states that she hasn't had good experiences with social workers in the past.

5. You approach the home of a family where you have an appointment to provide in-home family counseling. You see a group of six young men hanging out in the yard talking to each other. As you walk closer to them on the way to the front door, one of them appears to quickly put something in his back pocket and turns to look at you to see if you have noticed him.

3

∎ ∎ ∎

PREVENTION

Section 1. Assault Cycle, Interview Pointers

Section Goals:

- To introduce the phases leading up to and following a violent outburst.
- To assist students and social workers in recognizing the application of the assault cycle as a guide to responding to potentially violent clients.
- To provide interview strategies for deterring violence.

Getting Ready:

Watch the beginning segment from the movie *Nuts* (idea suggested by Dr. Suzanne McDevitt of Edinboro University, Pennsylvania) for a depiction of the assault cycle (Kaplan & Wheeler, 1993), which is explained below.

ASSAULT CYCLE

The best protection social workers have against behavior escalating to violence is good communication skills. We should not minimize the value of these skills that help clients feel less powerless, more able to express their feelings, and more able to see other options. When people feel that they are respected and understood, it is less likely that their hostility will grow and that they will resort to raging episodes (Blumenreich & Lewis, 1993).

Understanding the cycle of aggression may help us to readily recognize and intervene early to de-escalate mounting tension, irritability, and developing panic (Kaplan & Wheeler, 1983). Such knowledge is helpful in suggesting when to use de-escalating communications and when such skills may not be an effective means of achieving safety.

According to Kaplan and Wheeler (1983) in their article "Survival Skills for Working with Potentially Violent Clients," on which the following material is based, most occurrences of assault follow a predictable pattern of five consecutive phases:

1. *Triggering Phase*
All clients have a baseline for their normative behaviors. The triggering phase marks the first deviation from these baseline demeanors.

2. *Escalation Phase*
During this phase the client's behavior, speech, and emotions move further away from her or his normative expressions, becoming more apparent and intense. As the vehemence and agitation increase, the client will be less likely to respond rationally or be able to be redirected away from progressing escalation. It is important to intervene early on in this cycle, as soon as it becomes apparent that the client is behaving apart from her or his baseline. Active, nonjudgmental listening and problem solving, for example, may divert the client's agitation from escalating further. If the client is not calmed by talking, the worker may excuse herself or himself, ask for help, and follow agency guidelines. Many reported incidents have happened after social workers felt an intuition of growing danger but chose to handle the situation themselves by dismissing their feelings as trivial or indicative of personal weakness (Newhill, 1995).

3. *Crisis Phase*
In the crisis phase the client has become so pumped up physiologically and psychologically that she or he is not able or inclined to control hostile feelings and instead becomes verbally or physically aggressive. This is usually not a time when active listening and problem solving are effective means of intervention. Instead, attention must be directed toward the worker's own safety, the safety of the aggressing client, and the safety of other clients and workers.

4. *Recovery Phase*
The client begins to return to baseline behaviors, but this is not a certain progression. The client is still in a precarious state, and a return to the crisis phase may be easily activated. In this phase, errors are made by workers who assume that the crisis is over and who move too fast, inadvertently

34

triggering another violent episode. To support the recovery, the worker needs to pace interventions in response to the client's cues and reassure the client about her or his safety. Give the client time to de-escalate and avoid disapproving comments or exploring the reasons for and consequences of the behavior.

5. *Postcrisis Depression Phase*
   Here the client has returned to baseline behaviors or has dipped below to even more subdued behaviors. Mental and physical exhaustion take over the client, whose feelings of remorse and shame enable her or him to be more receptive to social work interventions. It may be appropriate to reflect on the assaultive episode with the client (Newhill, 1992), to help the client discuss the consequences of the behavior and deal with feelings of fear or guilt that someone got hurt, (Lanza, 1983) to understand the dynamics or events that preceded her or his losing control, and to consider appropriate choices and behavioral options for the future when she or he becomes anxious or angry (Lehmann, Padilla, Clark, & Loucks, 1983). If there was a precipitating problem that needs to be addressed, clarify that problem, explore alternative solutions, and evaluate these. Follow up on whatever decisions were made (Davies, 1989).

Points to Remember:

- The five phases of the assault cycle provide hints of how and when to use communication skills to de-escalate, and when such communications may not be helpful.
- It is important to intervene early in the assault cycle to defuse the situation and prevent further escalation.
- If a client is escalating toward the crisis phase and the worker's interventions have not defused the mounting aggression, the worker needs to focus on her or his safety and the safety of others present.
- Do not assume that the crisis is over until it is completely over. Stay alert.

Section 2. Interview Pointers

Section Goals:

- Provide interview strategies for deterring violence.
- Identify verbal communication skills for de-escalation purposes.

- Note nonverbal communications that can also be de-escalating.
- Focus on relationship variables that may prevent violence.
- Note the importance of calm and continuous thinking.
- Regard retreat as a legitimate strategy to prevent violence.
- Help students and social workers acknowledge the importance of responding to each situation on the basis of its unique conditions.
- Provide the opportunity for students and social workers to apply de-escalation interview strategies in a role-play.
- Distinguish responses that may escalate aggressive behaviors from those that defuse.

Getting Ready

- Organize fellow students or co-workers into small groups and prepare to conduct role-plays.
- Prepare to discuss the role-plays based on the responses to the **Interviewer Evaluation Form.**

INTERVIEW POINTERS

Many violence-prone individuals never explode, not because they don't have the capacity to but because they haven't encountered the interactive situation that would activate their eruption (Roberts, 1983). The most constructive way to deal with violence is to prevent it from happening in the first place (Blumenreich & Lewis, 1993). Generally the best way of doing this is to lessen the perceived threat and feelings of helplessness. We have learned that there usually is a cycle that predicts violent incidents, rather than violence erupting out of nowhere. Thus, social workers can often be alert to warning signs and intervene early, using communication skills to successfully prevent a violent outburst (Blumenreich & Lewis, 1993).

These interview skills, used in a manner that communicates acceptance, respect, and empathy, are suggested within the literature as ways to defuse hostility and anger and to protect the worker. Although there is no sure way to prevent violence, just as there is no way to always predict it, it is important to consider a variety of options so that one can pick and choose, thinking expansively and creatively in times of crisis.

1. De-Escalating Verbal Communication

Facilitate Expressing Feelings and Thoughts

When the client is expressing distress, the clinician can use the skills of active listening and reflecting the client's feelings in order to acknowledge those feelings and the client's right to experience them. This in itself may help to defuse a potentially volatile situation. Confirming a client's feelings validates the client as a worthy person. Furthermore, encapsulating the client's feelings encourages the client to ventilate and to examine her or his feelings and experiences. It is important to leave space that provides the client with sufficient opportunity to express herself or himself so that she or he doesn't have to explode or attack to be heard (Eichelman, 1995). Verbally expressing anger is more empowering and higher functioning than directing the aggression into physical acts (Star, 1984). By talking out angry feelings, the client may lessen their intensity and be reassured by the social worker's ability to cope with anger nondefensively.

Communicating empathy also involves paraphrasing the content of what the client says (Blumenreich & Lewis, 1993). Encapsulating clients' thoughts may help them to clarify their own thinking and identify the problem. Focusing on thinking rather than on feeling, if appropriately timed, may help the client move away from a volatile emotional state.

Since violence is often a momentary response, delay tactics make it less likely to occur (Blumenreich & Lewis, 1993). Careful listening and paraphrasing that engage the client in continuous, calm conversation create a de-escalating delay process.

Respond Succinctly

Verbal responses should be short, simple, to the point, and straightforward (Blumenreich & Lewis, 1993). Prolonged or rambling responses may be more confusing to a client whose overemotional state may be interfering with thought processing and may not come across as empathic and genuine. However, repetition may be necessary because an aroused client may have difficulty focusing and processing verbal messages that are said only once or twice (Eichelman, 1995).

Encourage Problem Solving

Using problem-solving skills helps the client break down a seemingly insurmountable problem into smaller tasks and consider nonviolent options.

Exploring options and noting choices, even if they are few, may have an empowering impact and eliminate the need for aggressive reactions (Blumenreich & Lewis, 1993). "What do you usually do to regain control when you get angry? Does walking help? Does talking help? Does writing a letter help?" (Hart, Broad, & Timborn, 1984).

Help the client to consider and brainstorm options for helpful ways to cope and for ways to address the problem triggering the anger. Violence-prone individuals have greater difficulty coming up with possible solutions to problems (Wainrib & Block, 1998). It might be appropriate to propose outright a suggestion for something the client can do, such as saying, "I'd be mad too, but you might consider doing this." If the client identifies a course of action or is given choices to choose from, the client may feel more pride and a sense of being in control.

Trying to meet reasonable requests will help to build rapport and empower the client (Hart, Broad, & Timborn, 1984). But, social workers must be careful not to make promises that cannot be kept, as this might stimulate retribution and interfere with the helping process (Eichelman, 1996).

Redirect

To redirect the client's emotions, choose to change the subject to funnel the client's attention away from an emotionally charged focus. For example, return to a previous success by stating, "You think the instructor was poor and so you had a hard time in the training session today, but I remember last week you felt very pleased about your learning. Can you recall what you learned then?" Later the client may indeed have to return to the material to which she or he is emotionally reactive and work through it, but at this time the client may immediately need to be focused in another direction in order to reestablish emotional control.

Eliminate Aggressive Responses

Macho, confrontational responses are generally not helpful and increase the likelihood of violence (Levy & Hartocollis, 1976). Defensive reactions, such as yelling, dominant body posturing, or setting unnecessary limits may aggravate aggressive behavior. A study that interviewed psychiatrists who had been attacked found that the victims pointed to having acted in a provocative manner before the attack, either by refusing a patient's request, forcing a patient to take medicine, or pushing the patient to deal with intra psychic material (Madden, Lion, & Penna, 1976). A study of a hospital unit that had only female nurses and nurses aides at night found virtually no incidents of violence, compared to wards employing both males and females (Levy & Hartocollis, 1976). Researchers attributed this finding to the nonconfrontational language and responses of women because of their socialization. Their ability to be self-aware and know when they are fearful and angry and how they typically respond to such circumstances, rather than blocking out such vulnerable feelings, enabled them to de-escalate aggression.

2. De-Escalating Nonverbal Communication

Just as with verbal interventions, nonverbal interventions can serve to communicate connectedness and attentiveness and be useful for staying aware, keeping safe, and moving the client toward de-escalation.

Physical Approach and Positioning

Do not approach the client from the back or head-on; rather, approach at an angle in order to be perceived as nonconfrontational (Blumenreich & Lewis, 1993). Avoid approaching the client too rapidly (Eichelman, 1995). Be careful not to isolate yourself with the client or turn your back to the client precipitously (Kronberg, 1983). Maintain appropriate physical distance so that the client would have to move in any attempt to lash out at you and also to ensure that the client will not misperceive aggression on your part (Kronberg, 1983).

Remember that individuals with a history of violence perceive a wider territorial space around themselves for a personal comfort zone than do others (Eichelman, 1995). Allow a potentially combative client five times the physical space that you would generally. Stand with your body at an angle to the client with your feet apart at hip width, with one foot more extended to the front than the other. This stance allows greater balance and mobility, while offering less of the body as a target for attack (Blumenreich & Lewis, 1993). Touching the client may be perceived as a challenge or arouse past incidents of trauma and traumatic reactions.

If a client is giving aggressive signals by invading your personal space, standing directly in front of you without much space in between, turn your body so that you are more at a right angle with the client. If the client resumes a confrontational stance, break the body symmetry in some way, such as shifting your weight to one leg and putting your hand to your chin. This will nonverbally signal that you are being friendly and that confrontation is not necessary (Davies, 1989).

Eye Contact

During a potentially violent situation, eye contact may be perceived as hostility and heighten aggressive arousal. Avoid staring (Davies, 1989). However, some eye contact may be helpful to convey interest and sincerity to the client and may also enable the social worker to be watchful. Often the client will glance in the direction where she or he will strike just prior to doing so (Blumenreich & Lewis, 1993).

Mirror Body Language

Join with the client's body language. For example, if a patient is sitting, then the worker should sit with legs and arms relaxed rather than crossed, to communicate openness and objectivity to the client.

Try to match enough with the client's affect and ardor in her or his nonverbal expressions in order to have influence in reducing their intensity (Eichelman, 1995). If the client is standing and nervously pacing and shouting, stand also and move while speaking somewhat more slowly and softly than the client. The idea here is to be enough in sync with the client in level and type of affect so that the client will perceive the social worker as allied with her or his feelings. Then as the social worker decreases the intensity, it is more likely that the client will also. As the client settles down, continue to recede and lead the client to lower levels of arousal. In contrast, if the client is shouting and the social worker is whispering, the client may perceive the social worker as being detached from her or his concerns and may respond by amplifying the behaviors.

3. Clarifying Relationship

Set Limits Appropriately

Many angry clients who might act out their anger actually fear losing control (Star, 1984). For these clients, having the social worker restating and holding to the limits may provide the needed external structure to help them keep their aggressive impulses at bay. To validate a client's feelings and express support, the worker may choose to say, "It's O.K. to be angry, it's not O.K. to strike out. What can I do to help you feel more in control right now?"

Firm limit setting can prevent clients from building momentum toward violent outbursts (Guy & Brady, 1998). Such expectations can communicate hope to a client that she or he in fact can exert self-control and is not helpless. The client who is fearful of losing self-control may be very reassured to be told enforceable limits will be upheld so that no harm comes to herself or himself or others (Blumenreich & Lewis, 1993). Limit setting involves indicating what is acceptable behavior and what is not and why it is unacceptable. The clinician also indicates what the consequences will be if the behavior continues (McNiel, 1998). The tone and wording involved in setting limits must affirm the client's self-esteem and not increase feelings of powerlessness (Hart, Broad, & Timborn, 1984).

Sometimes asking the client directly and repeatedly for the necessary behavior in an authoritative manner can be effective, such as saying, "Put down the chair!" The person may not always comply with the directive the first time it is stated but may do so after it is repeated (Davies, 1989).

Limits that cannot be enforced should not be introduced because ambiguous limits may invite assault (Eichelman, 1995). Limit setting may necessitate a clinical team approach rather than an individual one (McNiel, 1998). Sometimes a client may direct anger toward one team member in particular. In a team situation, the worker may be able to remove herself or himself so that other team members who are less negatively emotionally charged for a client can take over (D. Meyers, personal communication, March 25, 2000). To do so the worker might say something such as, "It seems like you are really distressed right now, so I'm going to let you talk with these people and move myself away so you won't get upset." The team would enforce limits after de-escalation techniques and communications had been tried and the client continued to escalate behaviors. A worker might say, "From what you said, you are telling us that you can't control yourself and we're going to help control you until you can do it by yourself." Such team enforcement should be carried out by professionals specifically trained in how to manage aggression.

Equalize Relationship

If violence springs from a sense of disequilibrium in power, then equality restores the client's sense of status and power. The worker can communicate in an assertive manner both verbally and nonverbally to avoid a power struggle and show respect for the client's dignity. Assertive communications are respectful but nonaggressive; they neither challenge nor relay submission, either of which may provoke attack (Kaplan & Wheeler, 1983). It is important not to come across in a parental voice that is authoritarian or lax, since either may stimulate poor controls in the client. "An honest straightforward approach within a structured here and now problem solving framework minimizes transference responses" (Star, 1984, p. 229).

Personalize or Depersonalize

If the aggression springs from associations with or transference to social workers, social workers should try to reveal a real person and not merely an enactment of a role (Davies, 1989). Use self-disclosure in a genuine way that is congruent with the topic and situation in order to bring the self to the forefront. For example, the worker might state, "I understand what you are saying because I also had a father who couldn't be satisfied no matter how hard we as children tried to please him."

In other situations communication skills can be used to clarify the worker's role. This may be critical if the client is confusing the worker with another person in her or his life. Clarify the social worker's role and repeat the program's intentions so that an emotionally aroused individual can attend to the message (Eichelman, 1995).

The worker might want to depersonalize the issue that is frustrating or enraging to the client. If an agency policy, for example, is dictating the worker's request or decision, then it might be important for the client to know this rather than thinking such a decision was at the worker's whim or directed toward her or him personally (Davies, 1989).

Use Self-Disclosure Purposefully

Sometimes social workers may try very hard to hide their fear so that a client will not suspect them of being afraid (Kronberg, 1983). Such attempts to cover up vulnerability may lead to incongruence between nonverbal and verbal expressions, inappropriate humor to mask fear, and misinterpretations that could lead to escalating behavior on the part of the client. Sometimes it is a reality check for the client to know that manifesting aggressive behavior is disconcerting and intimidating for others. If the client is determined to instill fear in the worker, however, she or he may increase threatening behaviors until the desired response is obtained. In such a case, the worker may be able to stop the behavior from escalating by use of self-disclosure, such as saying, "I wish you wouldn't do that; it really worries me" (Davies, 1989, p. 312). Such expressions of being uncomfortable should not imply either that the client will be allowed to act out threats or that the clinician is not able to hold her or him to appropriate behavioral limits (Eichelman, 1996).

Relate with Sensitivity to Diversity

Be aware of racial and ethnic issues and differences in order to be sensitive to and respectful of all clients. Take into consideration, for example, that there may be different cultural responses to crisis situations and to professional helpers (Wainrib & Block, 1998).

4. Staying Calm, Thinking

Communicate calmness verbally and nonverbally (Hart, Broad, & Timborn, 1984; McNiel, 1998). Keep an even, slow, soft-toned neutral voice and a confident, nonauthoritarian, nonjudgmental posture, so that the client feels reassured rather than pressured. When the client escalates toward the crisis state, the worker, whose adrenaline is also pumping, can similarly advance into a crisis state. A worker who also gets agitated and irritable may communicate an attitude of blame, provoking the client's aggression. Moreover, high anxiety can be provocative and interfere with good judgment and the ability to recognize appropriate options. It is important to keep anxiety in check by practicing various anxiety management techniques, such as deep breathing, self-talk, and soothing visualizations (Kaplan & Wheeler, 1983).

In some situations staying calm and relaxed may not be a realistic goal. However, no matter how agitated, the social worker still needs to keep thinking in order to review the possible options and choose the best one. Davies (1989) thinks it is highly unlikely that the worker will stay calm and suggests that it is more reasonable for the worker to aim for an attitude of, "No matter how agitated I feel, I am going to keep thinking and decide what is best to do" (p. 312).

5. Additional Strategies

Alter the Environment

Outbursts may be avoided by changing the environment so that the client can reestablish self-control: Direct the client to leave the immediate proximity, change the session to another room, or invite the client to have a snack. Changing the environment can have a calming effect, and offering food may be a soothing response that can reassure the client (Blumenreich & Lewis, 1993).

A strategy for altering the environment may be to separate clients from each other to remove fuel or an audience for the escalation of aggressive behaviors (Haber, Fagan-Pryor, & Allen, 1997).

Retreat

When the client is not de-escalating, continuing a heated interaction is likely to serve to increase the possibility of violence. Retreat can be a very professional and preventative action on the part of the worker. Telling the client, "I am leaving," and explaining why may be a way to disengage from the intense exchange (Blumenreich & Lewis, 1993). The following kinds of statements can be used: "I am leaving now because I think we can better discuss this at a later date." "I am going to get a file that will help me gain some information I need to address your concerns." "I can't help with that problem, but it is important to me, so I am going to get my supervisor who may be able to help."

Enable Client Means of Retreat

Furthermore, the worker can remind the client of her or his freedom to leave the room at any time, so that if the client reaches the excitement level of fight or flight, the client has the choice of exiting without incident.

Caveat

These strategies have been mentioned in clinical writings. However, there have not been outcome studies to verify that they are effective under certain circumstances. Thus, these responses can be considered as possible alternatives available to the practitioner for defusing a potentially assaultive situation. In all cases, nevertheless, the social worker should choose her or his responses based on professional and intuitive judgements that are sharply attuned to the particular situation. If the worker senses that a suggested strategy would make the situation more dangerous, it should not be employed. There is no predictably effective step-by-step prescription of how to respond to ensure safety. Instead, each situation requires a unique approach.

Points to Remember:

- Use verbal communication that helps the client restore a sense of status and control.
  - Help the client to talk out angry feelings rather than acting upon them.
  - Speak simply and repeat as necessary.
  - Help the client to overcome an insurmountable problem by breaking it down and exploring alternative solutions.
  - Redirect the client to move away from an issue that is overwhelming her or his inner controls.
  - Avoid aggressive responses.
- Use nonverbal communication that also de-escalates the situation.
  - Position yourself so that you are neither threatening nor an easy target.
  - Maintain eye contact that communicates involvement, not aggression.
  - Match your body language so that the client will follow your decrease in intensity.
- Relationship factors can encourage a decrease in the excitement level.
  - Provide a firm, supportive structure of limit setting.
  - Equalize the relationship through assertive communications.
  - Personalize or depersonalize yourself to lessen the danger.
  - Make appropriate disclosures to help the client connect with the reality of the situation.
  - Relate with sensitivity to diversity.
- Internally experience and project calm, if possible, but no matter what, keep thinking.
- Other interview strategies
  - Alter the environment.
  - Retreat as a strong preventative measure.
  - Allow the client the option of flight rather than fight.
- Select the intervention strategy based on your own intuition and assessment.

ROLE-PLAY EXERCISE

For this exercise, role-play a situation of potential violence in small groups with co-workers or fellow students. Ideas for the role-play include (Newhill,

1992): an angry, abusive spouse of a client confronts a worker about her or his interference in the client's marital relationship; a social worker informs an adolescent that she needs to go to a drug rehabilitation program; a social worker talks with a client about the need for hospitalization. A role-play can also be based on one of the case scenarios from chapter 2.

First, the person role-playing the social worker should show how *not* to intervene; then role-play effective application of knowledge of the assault cycle and communication skills. The person playing the client should not behave in a preset way, but rather should react in response to the worker's interventions. Observers of the second role-play should record what they witnessed using the **Interviewer Evaluation Form** found at the end of the chapter.

The questions on the **Interviewer Evaluation Form** can be used with everyone involved to help review the application of the information covered and bring closure to the exercise. For convenience the questions are reiterated below:

1. What were the cues that the client might become physically aggressive?
2. At what phase did the worker first intervene to interfere with the assault cycle?
3. What did the worker do in an attempt to defuse the situation?
4. What was the effectiveness of these interventions?
5. What are other alternatives for intervening in this situation?

INTERVIEW POINTERS

- Facilitate talking out feelings and thoughts
- Respond succinctly
- Encourage problem solving
- Redirect
- Eliminate aggressive responses
- Position yourself strategically
- Make eye contact carefully
- Mirror body language
- Set limits appropriately
- Equalize relationship
- Personalize or depersonalize
- Use self-disclosure purposefully
- Relate with sensitivity to diversity
- Stay calm, keep thinking
- Alter the environment
- Retreat
- Enable client means of retreat

INTERVIEW EVALUATION FORM

1. What were the cues that the client might become physically aggressive?

2. At what phase did the social worker first intervene to interfere with the assault cycle?

3. What did the social worker do in an attempt to defuse the situation?

4. How effective were these interventions?

5. What are other alternatives for intervening in this situation?

4

■ ■ ■

Environmental Safeguards and Response Planning

Section 1: Work Site Adaptations, a Response Plan, Agency Policies

Section Goals:

- To give examples of changes in the work site that may improve safety.
- To acquaint students and social workers with the possibility and benefit of response planning.
- To give examples of safety-oriented policies.
- To consider how these safety options are employed or could be employed in agencies.

Getting Ready:

Draw your work site, noting what features in the work environment are protective of safety and what others might facilitate violence. (If you are not currently employed as a social worker, you may want to make a general list of what workplace features result in a safe or an unsafe work environment.)

WORK SITE ADAPTATIONS

The nature of the setting can precipitate violence (Blumenreich & Lewis, 1993). Noise, disorganization, staff conflict, cold-appearing surroundings, crowding, isolated offices, lack of an alarm system, etc., can all contribute to the risk of combative explosions.

After you have drawn your work site, answer the questions "What do you notice about your work environment from a safety analysis point of view?" and "What in your work environment could be used as weapons?"

Workplace accommodations for safety vary according to the agency and should be selected based on the safety needs particular to the work site. Examples of these environmental precautions derived from *OSHA's Guidelines* (OSHA, 1996) and supplemented from the contemporary literature are:

1. *Possible Weapons*
   Be aware of items in the workplace that could be used as weapons or missiles and try to limit them. Potential weapons include vases, pictures, telephones, ashtrays, hot drinks, soda bottle, pens, etc. (McNiel, 1998; Schultz, 1987). Also, when interviewing potentially violent clients, remove clothing accessories that can be used in harmful ways; these include necklaces, dangling earrings, and neckties (McNiel, 1998).
2. *Alarm Systems and Other Security Devices*
   These may include panic buttons, hand-held or mounted buzzers, cellular phones, intercoms, etc. These emergency tools need to be tied to a dependable planned response system (Griffin, 1995).
3. *Metal Detectors*
   If weapons are detected, there must be a developed systematic response.
4. *Interview Rooms that Have Two Exits and Are in View*
   Offices should allow for two ways of exit. There might be a special interview room that also has a large window or one-way mirror to allow for viewing from the outside. Furthermore, offices should not be in secluded areas where no other practitioners are around to respond if needed.
5. *Pleasant Surroundings*
   Interview rooms and waiting rooms should be designed for comfort and stress reduction with attention to such features as soft lighting and calming color schemes, comfortable chairs, updated magazines, and toys (Kaplan & Wheeler, 1983).

6. *Furniture Arrangement*

Arrange furnishings in a way that allows for clients and staff to make quick exits and prevents entrapment (Kaplan & Wheeler, 1983). For example, placing the worker and client's chairs equidistant from the door would provide opportunity for either to leave without blocking the other. Chairs set at an angle may be conducive to a more supportive exchange, while chairs set head-on may prompt a more competitive one (Davies, 1989). A worker's chair that is lighter in weight could be picked up and used as a shield (Wainrib & Block, 1998).

RESPONSE PLANNING

Planning for "what if" situations needs to be an ongoing part of staff meetings and training and requires coordination and support of all employees and administrators. Here is a vignette that suggests how preventive planning can be implemented, based on material from Edelman (1978):

Imagine a potentially violent client walking into a mental health center waiting room. She is a young adult who is muttering to herself as she paces. She walks up to the receptionist, who can see the obvious tension in the woman's face and fists. The receptionist, along with everyone working at the agency, has attended safety training and knows agency policies pertaining to safety. He conducts his initial inquiry as briefly and calmly as possible. It is the receptionist's responsibility to direct the client to a space within the center that offers the maximum security options to the evaluating clinicians. He must alert the intake worker to the emergency situation without letting the client know that she is special by using a code. He says, "A client is here to see you. The front office next to the bathroom is free." The front office refers to an especially secure interview room with two exits and without objects that can be used as weapons.

When the intake worker receives the notification, he responds immediately by contacting a member of the senior staff, who will join him to present themselves to the client as the evaluative team. Next, the social worker alerts the clinic director so that she can telephone him after he has been interviewing the client for a few minutes. The director, by asking questions requiring yes or no answers, can determine whether the interviewers are in danger, whether the client has a weapon, whether the building should be evacuated, and whether she should call again. If the interviewers do not answer the phone, the director knows to call the police.

AGENCY POLICIES

Agency policies may prevent violent episodes. These selected suggestions come from *OSHA's Guidelines* (OSHA, 1996) as well as from a literature review:

1. Administrators make known to clients and workers that violence will not be tolerated.
2. All violent incidents are promptly reported to the worker's supervisor and recorded.
3. Initial interviews or intake evaluations are scheduled during times when many colleagues are usually present in the office. Workers are never alone in the office or building with an ongoing client who may potentially become combative (McNiel, 1998).
4. Strategies are in place for how workers can summon immediate help from co-workers. When possible, other staff members should be alerted to the possibility of violence occurring so that they can be ready to provide assistance (Beck & Roy, 1997). Workers can make use of panic buttons or have a coded message to communicate potential combativeness to the receptionist. These strategies are regularly reviewed and updated. There is a clear office understanding that acceptance of help from colleagues is okay.
5. Behavioral intervention plans for responding to possibly violent clients are in place. These include guidelines for personal behavior and contingency plans formulated for a range of intimidating circumstances. These plans address procedures for interviewing new or agitated clients, who in the agency should be notified, steps to take when weapons are present, and when and how it is advisable to call the police (Star, 1984). These procedures and plans could be changed, refined, and updated as further discussion, training, and needs arise (Davies, 1989).
6. Staff meetings, case management conferences, and safety training are used to discuss realistic scenarios and effective ways to handle potentially violent situations. Clinicians should not expect to effectively re-

spond during an attack without having cognitively rehearsed what they would do and say (Davies, 1989). Openly addressing safety issues in the course of agency business has the advantage of removing the shame and fear from this issue and keeping workers better prepared to handle threatening episodes (Guy & Brady, 1998). Workers are enabled to discuss when they feel unsafe and to suggest measures that can be adopted to improve safety precautions in the agency.

7. Social workers keep each other informed of potentially violent clients through notification in staff meetings and by systematically flagging violent clients' charts and attaching special messages to computer files in accordance with rules of confidentiality (Blumenreich & Lewis, 1993; Griffin, 1995; OSHA, 1996).

8. Workers interview "agitated clients in relatively open areas that still maintain privacy" (OSHA, 1996, p.6). It may, however, be necessary to leave the office door open with staff outside, or conduct the interview in the presence of other staff (McNiel, 1998).

9. Clients who must wait for service are treated in a courteous, respectful manner, and periodically notified of the wait and assured of their importance. Measures are implemented to reduce waiting time.

10. Staff coverage and presence are adequate, along with clarity of staff member's roles and predictability of schedules (Blumenreich & Lewis, 1993).

11. Procedures exist for how to support staff members who have been victims of violence and include a post-incident evaluation and provisions for affected staff to receive crisis counseling.

12. Safety training is provided to all personnel including line, support, and administrative staff. This training is integrated with and complementary to ongoing safety initiatives (Griffin, 1995).

ADVOCATE FOR SAFETY ISSUES

If a social worker is employed in an agency where safety issues or risk reduction training have not been given attention, this practitioner may wonder how to put these ideas into practice in the workplace. Although ways to advocate for safety measures within the workplace is a new area of consideration, some of the following ideas were generated in discussion with colleagues (L. Reeser, personal communication, January 3, 2000).

Social workers who realize the importance of safety may serve a central role in helping their agencies become proactive in developing violence prevention strategies. If a social worker becomes aware of the relevance of safety efforts through involvement in a disconcerting incident, this dangerous situation should be written up and presented to the appropriate administrator(s). She or he might also conduct an informal assessment survey among co-workers to determine their safety concerns and needs. Such a survey may ask about work circumstances that generate feelings of risk, client or problem situations that are red flags, and areas in which workers sense they need help. Such a survey could be conducted before or as part of a staff discussion that includes administrators. It is important to include administrators in discussions and in safety training because the commitment to develop a culture of safety must come from everyone.

If a social worker encounters administrative resistance to instituting safety measures and training, a formal proposal may be the next step. This proposal could include results from a more formal survey on the nature and number of risk factors staff confront during their work. Or a sample of case files could be reviewed to determine how many high risk factors are present in the client population. Information on how other local social service programs and agencies are supporting worker safety could be convincing. This manual might also give confirmation that safety concerns are legitimate issues for social service agencies to address. OSHA guidelines that suggest recommended professional standards for risk reduction may also give credibility and importance to the matter of worker safety. It might even be effective to include publicized cases in which social worker(s) encountered violence. Such a proposal with supporting materials could be presented to the appropriate administrator or agency board.

Students and schools of social work can also advocate for safety. A school could establish criteria for selecting field placement agencies that require them to honor and respect students' concerns about safety, and to provide students with safety training and information pertaining to their agencies' specific guidelines and policies. While the school may provide general safety training, the agencies could provide students with information particular to their specialized settings and client-problem situations. If the agency does not have safety policies and guidelines in place, the field director could work with the agency to develop these. Furthermore, the school could offer field instructors safety training or provide safety materials to them. Students could also share their safety awareness with their field instructors by initiating a review suggested by the **Agency Checklist for Worker Safety**.

CONSIDERATION OR GROUP DISCUSSION

Here are two proposals for consideration or group discussion concerning the information in this section:

1. Respond to the following three questions or discuss them with co-workers or fellow students:
   A. When do you feel unsafe in your field placement or work situation?
   B. What changes in policy or workplace environment could alleviate your discomfort?
   C. What strategies could you use for getting these changes implemented?
2. Consult the **Agency Checklist for Worker Safety** at the end of the chapter when considering or discussing the questions above.

Points to Remember:

- Adaptations can be made to the work site to improve safety.
- Response planning helps staff to alert and support each other.
- Agency policies can address safety concerns in a variety of ways and need to be suited to the specific agency.
- Awareness of these options enables practitioners to evaluate their work sites.

Section 2: Home Visits

Section Goals:

- To provide basic safety procedures for field visits.
- To develop students' and social workers' sense of responsibility for their own safety.

Getting Ready:

Based on the material presented so far, think about what additional steps may be taken to ensure social workers' safety during home visits.

HOME VISITS

This section includes suggestions about keeping safety in mind when preparing for and going out on a home visit. Because specific safety precautions should be tailored to the individual situation of the home visit, these are only suggested guidelines. Participants are encouraged to make additional recommendations.

Do Some Preparation

Determine where to meet the client and whether there is a need for accompaniment. Does the meeting really need to take place in the client's home, or would it be therapeutically acceptable to make contact in the office? (Davies, 1989) If there is a question of safety, consider whether the visit with the client should be held in the office or a public place such as a restaurant or library (Rey, 1996). Perhaps the situation calls for two workers or a worker and a supervisor. It might even necessitate that the worker be escorted by a police officer (Newhill & Wexler, 1997; Rey, 1996). Scalera (1995) cites an example of an agency that delineated circumstances under which caseworkers would be required to use a team approach for home visits after finding that a voluntary buddy system was not implemented consistently. Err on the side of safety, and when necessary discuss safety concerns with a supervisor.

Know the Client

The social worker should know as much as possible about the client prior to making a home visit. Read her or his file for a history of violence and risk factors for its recurrence (Newhill & Wexler, 1997). Examine whether the situation surrounding the home visit resembles previous precipitating events or triggers. Also reflect on whether there is something in the client's circumstances *that day* that might increase the probability of her or his acting violently (Davies, 1989).

Know the Environment

Perhaps a co-worker familiar with the area can be informative about potential dangers and helpful precautions. Providers already accepted in the client's neighborhood could be called upon to help foster the worker's safety (Newhill & Wexler, 1997). Or the client may meet the worker to accompany her or him through the neighborhood to the client's home (Rey, 1996).

Consider the time of day and the day of the week that would provide safety. It is important to note if there are others in the household who might present a risk of violence and whether drugs or weapons may be present. Judge who will likely be at the home during the visit and whether such a visit could be made at a time when a person who uses drugs or is prone to violence is away. Will an aggressive dog be in the yard or in the home? (Scalera, 1995) If possible, know where all of the entrances and exits to the meeting place are (Davies, 1989).

Communicate Appearance Wisely

Wear professional attire that will represent you as a nonthreatening person. Avoid wearing lots of jewelry and expensive clothing that will call attention to a newcomer in the environment (Smith College, n.d.). Don't wear shoes that will make it difficult to move quickly (Smith College, n.d.). Don't carry heavy notebooks, briefcases, or purses that could restrict movement or be a target for theft.

Plan for Connection with Colleagues

Be sure the agency knows the itinerary. Make location and approximate arrival and departure times clear (Rey, 1996). Consider the wisdom of planning for a routine call to the office at each visit or arranging to receive such a call (Davies, 1989). Specified code words could be helpful for communication with staff in such situations. A cellular phone programmed with agency and emergency numbers for quick dialing can be an important safety tool (Scalera, 1995).

Plan the route and travel on main roads (Smith College, n.d.). Ensure that the car has plenty of fuel so it will not run out of gasoline.

Conducting the Home Visit

Be alert to nonverbal cues. The social worker's nonverbal behavior should communicate that she or he knows where to go and what to do there, that she or he is not lost, and that she or he is neither timid nor imperious (Smith College, n.d.). Stay aware of persons in the vicinity (Smith College, n.d.). If people are loitering near the destination and seem threatening, the social worker may choose to pass by and return another time or day. Observe whether people have weapons or are wearing clothing in which weapons could easily be concealed.

Park in a place that allows quick escape. For example, don't park in the driveway where someone coming later could block the exit route.

When approaching the house, listen for any untoward sounds. If a noisy argument is in progress, leave and return another time. When ringing the doorbell or knocking, stand to the side of the door. The social worker must promptly and clearly identify herself or himself so as not to be mistaken for someone else.

Notice any hesitancy of the client(s) in opening the door. It may be an indication that the social worker should not enter (Smith College, n.d.). Do a quick visual scan of the room looking for any possible signs of danger, such as drugs or weapons. Be watchful of all persons; initially observe any signs of intoxication, withdrawal, abuse, or other threatening emotional or physical expressions. Learn who else besides the client is at home. If there are indications of threats to anyone's safety, promptly and politely ask to postpone the visit. Otherwise, note where the exits are and sit in the front room close to the door. The worker may also interview the client on the front porch or in the apartment foyer (Rey, 1996). If there is a change between the persons who were supposed to be in the home compared to those who are actually present, reassess whether the initial plans for the meeting are still safe and realistic or whether altered plans would be more useful (Davies, 1989). Stay alert. If there is a threat at a later point during the interview, courteously end the visit.

In addition to reviewing these guidelines, social workers may add other ideas to the list about how they will protect themselves. Sometimes gender roles or characteristics may interfere with observing cautionary measures. For example, women may try to overcompensate for female stereotypes connoting weakness, timidity, fearfulness, and need for protection, resulting in the abandonment of reasonable safety precautions. Conversely, men motivated to uphold stereotypical male characteristics of strength, courage, fearlessness, and aggression may forfeit prudent safety measures. Gender stereotypes within the work group could create expectations that male workers should obediently assume greater risks. Acknowledging and discussing such issues can communicate professional norms upholding the rights of all workers to take reasonable precautions to protect themselves.

Points to Remember:

- Home visits and traveling within communities require special safety precautions.

- Not all home visits should be made or made alone—options need to be considered when safety is a consideration.
- Prepare for a home visit with safety in mind:
  - read the file to determine risk factors
  - talk to informed colleagues
  - think about the area and setting of the home visit
  - keep others informed of your whereabouts.
- Be alert while carrying out the home visit.

AGENCY CHECKLIST FOR WORKER SAFETY

The following questions are for your consideration and possible discussion at your field placement or workplace. The goal is to plan for the safety of both workers and clients.

1. What written policy is there related to worker and client safety? (for example, orientation for staff and students).

2. What planning has staff undertaken for a situation where a worker feels uncomfortable or concerned about safety? (for example, staff in-service training, agreed-upon signals to obtain help, phone system, safety plan, periodic discussion).

3. How does the office arrangement contribute to or deter safety? (for example, location of desk, doors, windows, phone, potential weapons).

4. What guidelines are available to assess for potential violence in clients? (for example, a written checklist).

5. What is the system for reviewing difficult client situations? (for example, supervision, quarterly review, peer consultation).

6. What risk factors have agency staff members identified for this particular population and workplace?

This list was developed by Dr. Ineke Way, School of Social Work, Western Michigan University.

5

...

AFTERMATH OF VIOLENCE

Section 1: Workers' Feelings and What to Do

Section Goals:

- To acknowledge the impact of trauma on workers who have been attacked.
- To introduce responses that provide support for the victim and enhance safety procedures.

Getting Ready:

- Review what you know to be effective in responding to a trauma such as a death or violent act.
- Consider how an on-the-job trauma may entail different steps or coping responses.
- If possible, prepare to conduct a discussion with co-workers or fellow students about **The Case of C**, a vignette developed by Newhill (1995) and found at the end of the chapter.

Violence may impact workers differently depending on a number of factors, including whether there is any sustained injury or loss, the severity of the violence, the degree of terror and duration of the incident, the worker's perception of the level of threat and lack of personal control, the worker's role and involvement in the event, previous exposure to combative episodes, concurrent or previous intense stresses, stress management skills,

61

and the social support and interventions the worker receives in the aftermath of violence (Wolf, Leonhardi, Polancih, & Knight, 1994; Wykes & Whittington, 1998). Since the reaction to violence depends on perceptions, coping skills, interactions, and environmental responses and *not just on the violent episode alone*, responses can be highly individualistic.

Even though many violent incidents result in minor or no physical injury, there can still be a serious psychological impact on the worker. One study of assaulted nurses found that none had sustained a major injury and 60 percent had no physical injury, yet 10 days after the assault 25 percent were experiencing symptoms of trauma (Wykes & Whittington, 1998). Some workers may have traumatic stress reactions, some may have short-term anxiety reactions, and still others may have hardly any symptoms of stress (Wykes & Whittington, 1998). This cautions us not to judge the impact of a violent incident merely on the degree of resulting physical injury or loss.

Furthermore, it is likely that others besides the attacked worker will be affected by the violence. Certainly if co-workers witness the event, they will be affected by the traumatic incident. In addition, family members and co-workers who weren't present can be frightened for each other and for their own safety, experiencing impacts of secondary trauma (Wolf et al., 1994).

STAGES OF THE IMPACT OF VIOLENCE ON WORKERS

The three stages of the impact of violence on social workers as described by Wolf et al. (1994) are noted below along with supplemental information from other sources.

Stage One

When workers experience an attack, their sense of control and expectations of reality may be turned inside out. It is likely too much to cope with all at once, so workers experience shock, disbelief, denial, or numbness. Adrenaline likely has pumped through their bodies, increasing the heart rate and respiration and ridding the body of excess fluids for easier "flight or fight" through perspiration, urination, defecation, or vomiting, or a combination of these. Since the body used so much energy to achieve this keyed-up state, workers may be exhausted and need to rest after the crisis.

Stage Two

Often 24 to 48 hours after the violent incident workers have had time to think and become more consciously aware of what happened. Such awareness may be accompanied by surges of intense and fluctuating emotions including anger, rage, hypervigilance, jumpiness, fear, terror, grief, sorrow, confusion, helplessness, guilt, depression, or withdrawal. The lability and intensity of these emotions create an overwhelming sense of vulnerability.

Workers' imaginations may run wild, and they may experience flashbacks and intrusive thoughts or images about the assault (Wykes & Whittington, 1998). They may think of the event repeatedly and be fearful a similar event will recur.

Stage Three

In this stage workers seek to incorporate the event into their identities in a way that permits them to grow and function. Workers mourn their loss of their earlier sense of immortality, invulnerability, safety, trust in others, and control over their lives. They strive to assimilate their new view of reality, reevaluate their vulnerabilities and competencies, and transform the personal meaning of this event into a reconstructed or expanded identity. They may gain a sense of safety that encompasses the fragility of life and allows them to move on in their lives, perhaps with altered priorities or renewed appreciation for life.

THE IMPACT OF VIOLENCE ON SOCIAL WORKERS' EMOTIONAL WELL-BEING

Sometimes after incidents of violence workers are expected to take it in stride. However, there can be six significant emotional consequences of client violence:

1. *Feelings of Incompetence and Failure*
   Episodes of client violence often leave workers with a sense of failure and incompetence. If students or more inexperienced workers are those who are the targets, this can exacerbate feelings of self-doubt and erosion in incipient confidence (Guy & Brady, 1998).

2. *Feelings of Guilt and Shame*

Workers who have been victims of violence often feel regret and self-blame. They may believe that they should have been braver and more skilled and have prevented the attack (Brown, Bute, & Ford, 1986; Tully, Kropf, & Price, 1993).

3. *Sense of Personal Responsibility*

Though there are ways to take more safety precautions and be more aware and mindful of safety matters, a high accuracy rate in the prediction and prevention of violence seems to be beyond our current collective clinical powers. Yet often after an incident of violence, clinicians report that they should have better predicted the occurrence and acted in a more effective manner to have prevented it. Taking on this strong sense of personal responsibility for the attack gives way to shame, guilt, and the assumption of clinical error and incompetence (Guy & Brady, 1998).

4. *Angry Feelings*

Victims may feel anger or rage that the very persons whom they were trying to help responded by attacking them. No matter how well they professionally understand the dynamic reasons for the attack, they may still be angry because these angry feelings arise from the helplessness and fear they experienced. Social workers, believing that it is not professionally acceptable to have angry feelings against clients, may not express these feelings to colleagues or others.

5. *Sense of Vulnerability*

The realization that being seriously harmed was a real possibility leaves victims feeling helpless, fearful, and dramatically aware of the danger in their work situation. They may fear being victimized again and feel less motivated to work, and some may consider leaving their jobs or the profession (Guy & Brady, 1998; Newhill, 1995).

6. *Denial*

Workers may deny their emotional distress from the attack. This minimization is a protective reaction to block their feelings of helplessness and anxiety. It might be too hard for the worker to admit to her- or himself the danger of the work, the limits of clinical knowledge and competency, and the unpredictability and uncontrollability of client assault. While early use of denial and avoidance may help reduce a worker's reactivity enough so that she or he can begin to process the event, continued use of denial may get in the way of psychological healing. Denial can interfere with the worker's understanding of the full impact of the incident and eliciting the help of others to process and resolve the trauma (Guy & Brady, 1998; Wykes & Whittington, 1998).

Besides these emotional reactions to violent incidents, others cited in the literature include emotional numbness, detachment, depression, paranoia, nightmares, increased concern of loved ones for their safety, marital discord, and a reduction in general emotional well-being (Guy & Brady, 1998; Wykes & Whittington, 1998).

THE IMPACT OF VIOLENCE ON WORKERS' BEHAVIORAL RESPONSES

1. *Behavioral Responses to Denial*
   If denial is operating, workers may underestimate their physical and emotional wounds and seek to assure colleagues, family members, and the client assailant that the attack had little consequence. They may not talk about the violent incident, may return to work prematurely, or may eagerly take on the most difficult clients (Guy & Brady, 1998).

2. *Protective Measures*
   Sometimes workers who have suffered an attack will refuse to see clients whom they consider to be prone to violence. During intake interviews they are more likely to screen for the potential for future violence (Guy & Brady, 1998). Furthermore, some studies suggest that following a violent incident many clinicians immediately transfer the violent client to another worker or terminate with that client (Guy, Brown & Poelstra, 1990).

   However, other studies show that 60 to 75 percent of clinicians did not become more selective about whom they were willing to work with after the occurrence of a violent incident (Guy & Brody, 1998). Worker victims of client violence were motivated to take steps to increase their personal safety. For example, they were more likely to attend safety training, develop a plan for obtaining assistance in a similar situation, avoid working alone, clarify during the start of treatment what client behaviors would not be tolerated, and make sure that their home address and number were not listed in the phone book.

WHAT TO DO

After an incident of violence, apart from responding to the client(s), there are suggested actions for both helping the victims and for learning from the occurrence how to improve safety measures. Here are nine actions that the victims and others can take:

1. *Admit that Violence Occurred*
   The victimized worker needs to acknowledge to her- or himself and others that violence occurred. Often the worker will minimize or ignore the seriousness of the incident (Blumenreich & Lewis, 1993; Guy & Brady, 1998).

2. *Crisis Intervention*
   Crisis intervention and counseling within 24 to 72 hours may help the victimized worker(s) to begin the recovery process, understand the event and its impact, and build a sense of control and safety (Wolf et al., 1994).
   - Encourage the victimized workers to verbalize their powerful feelings and recreate their experiences.
   - Normalize their felt reactions by telling them that others experiencing such a traumatic event would also have stress reactions.
   - Alert the workers to the possible emotional intensity and crisis reactions they may subsequently experience. Preparing them for this potential outbreak allows them to feel more mastery, lessening the self-doubt and confusion that might beset them if these symptoms arise without forewarning.
   - Help them strategize about ways to cope with the symptoms and painful thoughts and feelings they may experience. Explore how they coped with past crises, discuss how they might do so this time, and offer additional ways to cope.

3. *Opportunity to Work through Feelings and Reactions*
   It is essential that the victim talk (within the bounds of confidentiality) about what happened as soon as possible in order to verbalize feelings and gain perspective (Wolf et al., 1994). Some victims are secretive about the fact that a violent incident took place. This deprives them of talking over the experience and getting the necessary support, ventilation of feelings, and reality clarification (Guy & Brady, 1998). Assaulted workers who were surveyed viewed their colleagues as being most understanding since they dealt with similar situations (Smith & Nursten, 1998).

Secondly, supervisors and family members were regarded as helpful. Other persons who may be helpful include personal therapists, members of the clergy or spiritual counselors, and confidantes. It is important that the victim not withdraw from her or his support network (Wolf et al., 1994).

4. *Support the Victim*

It is critical that other staff members show support for the victim in order to counter possible feelings of shame and demoralization. Compassion, availability, and patience will be helpful to clients working through victimization. Insensitive responses may have the impact of victimizing workers again through what is known as secondary trauma. Initial attitudes and comments that communicate blame will not help the worker's healing (Wolf et al., 1994). It is also important not to use inappropriate humor or minimize the impact of the experience, such as flippantly remarking, "What do you expect?" (Smith & Nursten, 1998).

5. *Report Writing*

Writing a report about the incident may not only serve documentation purposes but also help the worker to further conceptualize and understand the incident.

6. *Removal of Stigma*

There needs to be an agency culture that communicates to workers that it is acceptable and part of professional behavior to seek support and professional counseling to work through psychological responses to threatening events that take place in the work context. The worker must take initiative to obtain any professional counseling necessary to satisfactorily resolve the trauma.

7. *Counseling for Others*

Loved ones of the victimized worker may be encouraged to get counseling to help them understand the worker's traumatic reactions and the recovery process, as well as to deal with their own anxieties (Wolf et al., 1994).

In therapeutic settings or groups it may be useful to allow other clients to ventilate, express any concerns about their own safety, and discuss appropriate behavior (Beck & Roy, 1997).

8. *Review*

Post-trauma discussion needs to thoughtfully review the circumstances surrounding the incident in order to identify specific safety needs and plan for future supports. How did staff handle the incident, including recognition of early warning signals, timing, and nature of responses to the client(s)? What did and did not work and why? (Madden, 1983).

Such discussion should inform safety training efforts, agency policies, and intervention plans for working with the client who aggressed and with other potentially violent clients.

9. *Other Considerations*

Treatment planning for the assailant client needs to include an assessment of the severity of the incident, the extent of contextual frustration or provocation, and causes of the violent behavior. Planning needs to consider what if any contact the assaulted worker will have with the client assailant and whether the client needs to be quickly transferred to another clinician.

Consideration may need to be given to whether the experience leaves the worker temporarily impaired and unable to provide the same quality service as previously.

EXERCISE

Read the **The Case of C** vignette (Newhill, 1995) aloud in small groups or alone and discuss or consider these five questions:

1. What do you think are the feelings and thoughts of the victim?
2. How do you regard this victim?
3. What response from co-workers and administrators would be (a) healing or (b) further victimizing?
4. What agency policies and provisions would be helpful to those social workers who are victims of violence?
5. What strategies could you use as a worker in an agency to have these policies incorporated?

Points to Remember:

- The nature of the reaction to a violent incident depends on many variables.
- There are stages of dealing with traumatic stress.
  - Workers who are victims of violence may feel a sense of failure, guilt, self-blame, anger, or fear and may use denial.
  - Workers may exhibit behavioral responses.
  - Crisis intervention may be necessary.

- Analyzing the traumatic event offers the opportunity for infusing safety awareness into the agency and for improving safety measures.
- Personal reactions among staff members along with agency policies may support recovery or interfere with healing and growth.

THE CASE OF C*

C, a 26-year-old white man, had a long history of assaultive and explosive behavior, including convictions for rape and attempted murder. While on parole, C came to the emergency room stating that he wanted help because he felt like hurting himself or someone else but refused to say what he might do "because it is too disgusting." In talking with the social worker, he was calm and spoke in a slow, soft voice but appeared extremely tense, as if he might explode at any time. C rejected an offer of psychotherapy, did not ask for hospitalization, and wanted to see a psychiatrist for medicine because "a psychiatrist is more qualified to change my life for me." The psychiatrist gave him a prescription for Mellaril (thioridazine hydrochloride).

C returned the following night in a rage because the Mellaril was not "working." He would not say what he wanted or needed and talked only about wanting to beat people's heads in—"yours, too, and that stinking doctor." When asked if he wanted to talk with the doctor about the medication, he said, "I'll be out in the lobby, and when you get your shit together you come find me," and stalked out. When called, he was nowhere to be found.

Over the next few weeks, C followed the social worker in his car. The police were notified but said they could do nothing. Twice the social worker received telephone calls at home in which an unidentified man threatened to kill him; the social worker thought it sounded like C's voice. Finally, after three weeks, the following and phone calls ceased. C never returned to the emergency room. The social worker, however, continued to feel anxious and feared his life was in danger.

Newhill, C. E. (1995). Client violence toward social workers: A practice and policy concern for the 1990s. *Social Work, 40*(5), 631–636.

REFERENCES

Beck, P. R., & Roy, R. (1997). Assaultive and destructive behaviour in a treatment setting: Guidelines for the psychiatrist. *Canadian Journal of Psychiatry, 42*(4), 987–989.

Binder, R. L., & McNiel, D. E. (1990). The relationship of gender to violent behavior in acutely disturbed psychiatric patients. *Journal of Clinical Psychiatry, 51,* 110–114.

Blumenreich, P & Lewis, S. (1993). *Managing the violent client: A clinician's guide.* New York: Brunner/Mazel.

Boettcher, E. G. (1983). Preventing violent behavior—an integrated theoretical model for nursing. *Perspectives in Psychiatric Care, 21*(2), 54–58.

Bouza, A. V. (1993, December 27). We are the enemy. *In These Times,* pp. 20–22.

Brown, R., Bute, S., & Ford, P. (1986). *Social workers at risk: The prevention and management of violence.* Hampshire, England: Macmillan.

Carmel, H., & Hunter, M. (1991). Psychiatrists injured by patient attack. *Bulletin of the American Academy of Psychiatry and the Law, 19,* 309–316.

Chaimowitz, G. A., & Moscovitch, A. (1991). Patient assaults on psychiatric residents: The Canadian experience. *Canadian Journal of Psychiatry, 36,* 107–111.

Davies, W. (1989). Prevention of assault on professional helpers. In K. Howells & C. R. Hollin (Eds.), *Clinical approaches to violence* (pp. 311–328). West Sussex, England: John Wiley & Sons.

De Becker, G. (1997). *The gift of fear: Survival signals that protect us from violence.* Boston: Little, Brown.

Eddy, S. (1998). Risk management with the violent patient. In P. M. Kleespies (Ed.), *Emergencies in mental health practice: Evaluation and management* (pp. 217–231). New York: Guilford Press.

Edelman, S. (1978). Managing the violent patient in a community mental health center. *Hospital and Community Psychiatry, 29*(7), 460–462.

Eichelman, B. S. (1995). Strategies for clinical safety. In B. S. Eichelman & A. C. Hartwig (Eds.), *Patient violence and the clinician* (pp. 139–154). Washington, DC: American Psychiatric Press.

Eichelman, B. S. (1996). Violent patients. In E. Jerome, V. Vaccaro, & G. Clark, Jr. (Eds.), *Practicing psychiatry in the community: A manual* (pp. 277–292). Washington, DC: American Psychiatric Press.

Estroff, S. E., Zimmer, C., Lachicotte, W. S., & Benoit, J. (1994). The influence of social networks and social support on violence by persons with serious mental illness. *Hospital and Community Psychiatry, 45,* 669–679.

Farber, B. A. (1983). Psychotherapists' perceptions of stressful patient behavior. *Professional Psychology: Research and Practice, 14,* 697–705.

Flannery, Jr., R. B., & Penk, W. E. (1996). Program evaluation of an intervention approach for staff assaulted by patients: Preliminary inquiry. *Journal of Traumatic Stress, 9*(2), 317–324.

Gil, D. G. (1996). Preventing violence in a structurally violent society: Mission impossible. *American Journal of Orthopsychiatry, 66*(1), 77–84.

Griffin, W. V. (1995). Social worker and agency safety. In R. L. Edwards (Ed.), *Encyclopedia of social work* (19th ed., Vol. 3, pp. 2293–2305). Washington, DC: NASW Press.

Guy, J. D., & Brady, J. L. (1998). The stress of violent behavior for the clinician. In P. M. Kleespies (Ed.), *Emergencies in mental health practice: Evaluation and management* (pp. 398–417). New York: Guilford Press.

Guy, J. D., Brown, C. K., & Poelstra, P. L. (1990). Who gets attacked? A national survey of patient violence directed at psychologists in clinical practice. *Professional Psychology: Research and Practice, 21,* 493–495.

Haber, L. C., Fagan-Pryor, E. C., & Allen, M. (1997). Comparison of registered nurses' and nursing assistants' choices of intervention for aggressive behaviors. *Issues in Mental Health Nursing, 18,* 113–124.

Hart, C. A., Broad, J., & Timborn, S. (1984). Managing violence in an inpatient setting. In S. Sanders, A. M. Anderson, C. A. Hart, & G. M. Rubenstein.(Eds.), *Violent individuals and families: A handbook for practitioners* (pp. 164–197). Springfield, IL: Charles C. Thomas.

Hatti, S., Dubin, W., & Weiss, K. (1982). A study of circumstances surrounding patient assaults on psychiatrists. *Hospital and Community Psychiatry, 38*(8), 660–661.

Kaplan, S. G., & Wheeler, E. G. (1983, June). Survival skills for working with potentially violent clients. *Social Casework, 64*(6) pp. 339–346.

Kemper, V. (1993, March/April). A tough cop on the trail of hope. *Utne Reader,* pp. 70–76.

Kronberg, M. E. (1983). Nursing interventions in the management of the assaultive patient. In J. Lion and W. Reid (Eds.), *Assaults within psychiatric facilities* (pp. 225–238). New York: Grune & Stratton.

Lanza, M. L. (1983). The reactions of nursing staff to physical assault by a patient. *Hospital & Community Psychiatry, 34*(1), 44–47.

Lehmann, L., Padilla, M., Clark, S., & Loucks, S. (1983). Training personnel in the prevention and management of violent behavior. *Hospital & Community Psychiatry, 34*(1), 40–43.

Levy, P., & Hartocollis, P. (1976). Nursing aides and patient violence. *American Journal of Psychiatry, 133*(4), 429–431.

Lidz, C. W., Mulvey, E. P., & Gardner, W. (1993). The accuracy of predictions of violence to others. *Journal of the American Medical Association, 8,* 1007–1011.

Link, B. G., Andrews, H., & Cullen, F.T. (1992). The violent and illegal behavior of mental patients reconsidered. *American Sociological Review, 57,* 275–292.

Madden, D. J. (1983). Recognition and prevention of violence in psychiatric facilities. In J. Lion and W. Reid, *Assaults within psychiatric facilities* (pp. 213–223). New York: Grune & Stratton.

Madden, D. J., Lion, J. R., & Penna, M. W. (1976). Assaults on psychiatrists by patients. *American Journal of Psychiatry, 113*(4), 422–425.

McNiel, D. E. (1998). Empirically based clinical evaluation and management of the potentially violent patient. In P. M. Kleespies (Ed.), *Emergencies in mental health practice: Evaluation and management* (pp. 95–116). New York: Guilford Press.

McNiel, D. E., & Binder, R. L. (1995). Correlates of accuracy in the assessment of psychiatric inpatients' risk of violence. *American Journal of Psychiatry, 152,* 901–906.

McNiel, D. E., Sandberg, D. A., & Binder, R. L. (1998). The relationship between confidence and accuracy in clinical assessment of psychiatric patients' potential for violence. *Law and Human Behavior, 22*(6), 655–669.

Newhill, C. E. (1992). Assessing danger to others in clinical social work practice. *Social Service Review, 66*(1), 64–84.

Newhill, C. E. (1995). Client violence toward social workers: A practice and policy concern for the 1990s. *Social Work, 40*(5), 631–636.

Newhill, C. E., Mulvey, E. P., & Lidz, C. W. (1995). Characteristics of violence in the community by female patients seen in a psychiatric emergency service. *Psychiatric Services, 46,* 785–789.

Newhill, C. E. & Wexler, S. (1997). Client violence toward children and youth services social workers. *Children and Youth Services Review, 19*(3), 195–212.

Norris, D. (1990). *Violence against social workers.* London: Jessica Kingsley Publishers.

Occupational Safety & Health Administration [OSHA] (1996). Guidelines for preventing workplace violence for health care and social service workers. *OSHA, 3148,* 1–10.

Ray, C. L., & Subich, L. M. (1998). Staff assaults and injuries in a psychiatric hospital as a function of three attitudinal variables. *Issues in Mental Health Nursing, 19,* 277–289.

Rey, L. D. (1996). What social workers need to know about client violence. *Families in Society: The Journal of Contemporary Human Services, 77*(1), 33–39.

Roberts, A. R. (1983). *Social work in juvenile and criminal justice settings.* Springfield, IL: Charles C Thomas.

Scalera, N. R. (1995). The critical need for specialized health and safety measures for child welfare workers. *Child Welfare, 74*(2), 337–350.

Schultz, L. G. (1987). The social worker as a victim of violence. *Social Casework: The Journal of Contemporary Social Work, 68,* 240–244.

Schultz, L. G. (1989). The victimization of social workers. *Journal of Independent Social Work, 3*(3), 51–63.

Sheridan, M., Henrion, R., Robinson, L., & Baxter, V. (1990). Precipitants of violence in a psychiatric inpatient setting. *Hospital and Community Psychiatry, 41*(7), 776–780.

Smith College School for Social Work. (n.d.). Safety tips for students in the field. Northampton, MA: Author.

Smith, M., & Nursten, J. (1998). Social workers' experience of distress—Moving toward change? *British Journal of Social Work, 28,* 351–368.

Star, B. (1984). Patient violence/therapist safety. *Social Work, 29,* 225–230.

Tardiff, K. (1997). Evaluation and treatment of violent patients. In D. M. Stoff, J. Breiling, J. D. Maser, & National Institute of Mental Health (Eds.), *Handbook of antisocial behavior* (pp. 445–553). New York: John Wiley & Sons.

Tully, C. T., Kropf, N. P., & Price, J. L. (1993). Is field a hard hat area? A study of violence in field placements. *Journal of Social Work Education, 29*(2), 191–199.

Tyron, G. S. (1986). Abuse of therapists by patients: A national survey. *Professional Psychology Research and Practice, 17* (4), 357–363.

Wainrib, B. R., & Bloch, E. L. (1998). *Crisis intervention and trauma response.* New York: Springer.

Whitman, R., Armao, B., & Dent, O. (1976). Assault on the therapist. *American Journal of Psychiatry, 133*(4), 426–429.

Wistedt, B., & Freeman, A. (1994). Aggressive patients. In F. M. Dattilio & A. Freeman, *Cognitive-behavioral strategies in crisis intervention.* **00–00.** New York: Guilford Press.

Wolf, K. L., Leonhardi, M., Polancih, D., & Knight, M. (1994). Helping employees recover from the trauma of workplace violence. *EAP Digest,* March/April, 26–28.

Wykes, T., & Whittington, R. (1998). Prevalence and predictors of early traumatic stress reactions in assaulted psychiatric nurses. *Journal of Forensic Psychiatry, 9*(3), 643–658.

Index

Security Risk: Preventing Client Violence against Social Workers

Cover design by Metadog Design Group

Interior design and composition by Cynthia Stock, Electronic Quill

Typeset in Adobe Garamond and Trajan

Printed by Victor Graphics,Inc.

CRITICAL PERSONAL SAFETY GUIDELINES AND ETHICAL PRACTICE TOOLS FROM NASW PRESS

Security Risk: *Preventing Client Violence against Social Workers,* *by Susan Weinger.* Research indicates that at least a quarter of professional social workers will confront a violent situation on the job. Half of all human services professionals will experience client violence at some point during their careers. *Security Risk* presents rational approaches for implementing safety guidelines in the social work environment. This invaluable manual provides easily applied methods and strategies for enhancing personal safety while remaining aware of the supportive, empathetic role of social workers.

ISBN: 0-87101-321-5. Item #3215. March 2001. 92 pages. $21.99.

The Social Work Ethics Audit: *A Risk Management Tool, by Frederic G. Reamer. The Social Work Ethics Audit* provides practitioners with a practical and easy-to-use tool that helps assess the adequacy of ethics-related policies, practices, and procedures related to clients, staff, documentation, and decision-making. Designed to work seamlessly with the audit instrument and computer disk, the accompanying text assists respondents in determining appropriate action steps and strategy to correct any inadequacies or lapses in ethical practices.

ISBN: 0-87101-328-2. Item #3282: Book with Word for Windows disk; Item #3282A: Book with Macintosh disk. March 2001. 88 pages. $39.99.

Current Controversies in Social Work Ethics: *Case Examples, by NASW Code of Ethics Revision Committee, Frederic Reamer, Chairperson.* Presents a cross-section of real examples of ethics dilemmas faced by social workers in contemporary practice situations. A companion work to the NASW *Code of Ethics,* this practical and thought-provoking handbook offers commentaries of related considerations and implications that helps the reader untangle the controversies and competing values associated with ethical decision-making.

6" x 9" pamphlet. Item #3002. 1998. 100 pages. $8.50.

Global Crisis of Violence: *Common Problems, Universal Causes, Shared Solutions, by Dorothy Van Soest.* This book sets forth the concepts of violence in systemic terms in the context of culture and institution. You'll learn how preventive investments in social infrastructures can provide fiscally and ethically sound solutions. An important text for Human Behavior in the Social Environment courses and for policy courses.

ISBN: 0-87101-276-6. Item #2766. 1997. 320 pages. $35.95.

Prudent Practice: *A Guide for Managing Malpractice Risk, by Mary Kay Houston-Vega and Elane M. Nuehring with Elisabeth R. Daguio.* Social workers and other human service professionals face a heightened risk of malpractice suits in today's litigious society. The NASW Press offers practitioners a complete practice guide to increasing competence and managing the risk of malpractice. Included in the book and on disk are 25 sample forms and 5 sample fact sheets to distribute to clients.

ISBN: 0-87101-267-7. Item #2677: Book with Word for Windows disk; Item #2677A: Book with Macintosh disk. 1996. 332 pages. $42.95.

The Legal Environment of Social Work, *by Leila Obier Schroeder.* This book focuses on the legal system as it influences the social work profession and highlights the laws that affect the delivery of social work services. Covers the criminal justice system, juvenile courts, marriage and filiation and adoption concerns, and legislation such as the American with Disabilities Act.

ISBN: 0-87101-235-9. Item #2359. 1995. 382 pages. $34.95.

(Order form and information on reverse side)

ORDER FORM

Qty.	Title	Item #	Price	Total
___	Security Risk	3215	$21.99	_____
___	The Social Work Ethics Audit			
___	Book with Windows disk	3282	$39.99	_____
___	Book with Macintosh disk	3282A	$39.99	_____
___	Current Controversies in SW Ethics	3002	$8.50	_____
___	Global Crisis of Violence	2766	$35.95	_____
___	Prudent Practice			
___	Book with Windows disk	2677	$42.95	_____
___	Book with Macintosh disk	2677A	$42.95	_____
___	Legal Environment of Social Work	2359	$34.95	_____

POSTAGE AND HANDLING
Minimum postage and handling fee is $4.95.
Orders that do not include appropriate postage
and handling will be returned.

DOMESTIC: Please add 12% to orders under $100
for postage and handling. For orders over $100
add 7% of order.

CANADA: Please add 17% postage and handling.

OTHER INTERNATIONAL: Please add 22% postage and
handling.

Subtotal	_____
Postage and Handling	_____
DC residents add 6% sales tax	_____
MD residents add 5% sales tax	_____
Total	_____

❒ **Check** or **money order** (payable to NASW Press) for $ _____.

❒ **Credit card**
   ❒ NASW Visa* | ❒ Visa | ❒ NASW MasterCard* | ❒ MasterCard | ❒ Amex

_____   _____

Credit Card Number   Expiration Date

Signature _____

Use of these cards generates funds in support of the social work profession.

Name_____

Address _____

City _____ State/Province _____

Country _____ Zip _____

Phone _____ E-mail _____

NASW Member # (if applicable) _____

(Please make checks payable to NASW Press. Prices are subject to change.)

NASW PRESS
P. O. Box 431
Annapolis JCT, MD 20701
USA

Credit card orders call
1-800-227-3590
(In the Metro Wash., DC, area, call 301-317-8688)
Or fax your order to 301-206-7989
Or order online at http://www.naswpress.org

Visit our Web site at http://www.naswpress.org.   3215BC